350
6/21

D0064851

Jon —

INSPIRE
OTHERS !

BLOOM

Inspiring Ownership at Work

Matt Dahlstrom

Bloom
Inspiring Ownership at Work
By Matt Dahlstrom
Drawing Board Publishing

Published by Drawing Board Publishing, LLC,
Copyright ©2014 Matt Dahlstrom
All rights reserved.

No part of this publication may be reproduced, stored in a retrieval system, or transmitted in any form or by any means, electronic, mechanical, photocopying, recording, scanning, or otherwise, except as permitted under Section 107 or 108 of the 1976 United States Copyright Act, without the prior written permission of the Publisher. Requests to the Publisher for permission should be addressed to Permissions Department, Drawing Board Publishing, LLC, 9249 S. Broadway #200 PMB 265, Highlands Ranch, CO 80129, permissions@bloom-book.com.

Limit of Liability/Disclaimer of Warranty: While the publisher and author have used their best efforts in preparing this book, they make no representations or warranties with respect to the accuracy or completeness of the contents of this book and specifically disclaim any implied warranties of merchantability or fitness for a particular purpose. No warranty may be created or extended by sales representatives or written sales materials. The advice and strategies contained herein may not be suitable for your situation. You should consult with a professional where appropriate. Neither the publisher nor author shall be liable for any loss of profit or any other commercial damages, including but not limited to special, incidental, consequential, or other damages.

Interior design and layout: Davis Creative – www.daviscreative.com

Library of Congress Control Number: 2013948581

ISBN: 978-0-9898749-0-8

ATTENTION CORPORATIONS, UNIVERSITIES, COLLEGES AND PROFESSIONAL ORGANIZATIONS: Quantity discounts are available on bulk purchases of this book for educational, gift purposes, or as premiums for increasing magazine subscriptions or renewals. Special books or book excerpts can also be created to fit specific needs. For information, please contact Drawing Board Publishing, LLC9249 S. Broadway #200, PMB 265, Highlands Ranch, CO 80129; orders@bloom-book.com.

For Joey

Thanks for helping me become an *Owner*.

TABLE OF CONTENTS

FOREWORD

The concept of owning something is an easy one to understand. It's human in nature; either you own something or you don't. Either you're connected with it or you're not. Either you are committed...or you're not. To explain this in words that others will be motivated by and moved enough to change their course of action is an entirely different story. That's an art—one where Matt Dahlstrom excels.

I have worked in an industry that understands the human factor of success—that without people, companies cannot succeed. It is this common bond between Matt and I that goes deep into the night while enjoying the combined love we both share—beer. In all the years working with others to inspire them to make a difference at work, it wasn't until Matt put what we wanted into words that things became fluid for the organization my father founded in 1928.

When I was first looking for outside help for my company, I interviewed five people but chose Matt Dahlstrom only to find out that I didn't choose him...he chose us. Matt works with only ten organizations per year and we were already on his short list. When I researched to see how he had performed for others, I wasn't surprised to hear them say, "Our Company is better today because Matt showed us how to inspire ownership." I spoke with one company Matt had consulted with and asked why they brought in Matt. He response was classic Kentucky, "When I took this job I found my hunting dogs were spending a lot of time sleeping on the front porch. Matt got them out in the field where they belonged."

Matt is a great motivator, communicator and facilitator. He is just as much at ease working a room of 2500 as he is with a room of 20. He has a unique ability to read the needs of people and help them achieve their goals. His communication style is to speak the truth—fortunately, he continues that in this book through what he calls "truth grenades"—effective reminders of what needs to be done spoken plainly, truthfully and told only in a way that he can deliver. *Bloom* is not only an enjoyable read it will make you and your company better on multiple levels. The book lends credence to the assertion that service requires motivation. Motivation can only be optimized if one is truly invested and that investment demands one thing—individuals take ownership at work.

Jack Vukelic

Director of Corporate Development

Try-it Distributing Co., Inc.

Buffalo, NY

ACKNOWLEDGMENTS

Writing is personal. It is a moment in time when you find the rhythm flowing from thought to words to paper.

Often times you get stuck—really stuck.

For all the people I looked to help me get unstuck:
E. Scott Forbes, Patrick Longo, Janica Smith,
Michael Olsson, Lindsay Dahlstrom, Harry Dahlstrom,
and the cutie from the marketing department, Ambryn.

Thank you.

INTRODUCTION

O N E of your employees comes to work and performs well; but when it comes down to it, he does nothing more than necessary. He'll get the job done, sure. However, his passion, his obsession, is not at work; it's on the golf course. He'll play shot after shot until darkness falls. Why? He sees how his improvement with his 5-iron can help him better fulfill *his* goal, which is to lower his handicap from ten to seven. He's never satisfied with his game. That's why he spends extra time improving all aspects of his swing, his putting, and his short game. But when the clock at work strikes 5:00, he's the first one out the door...likely on his way to the driving range.

In the kitchen, another employee may work deep into the night in an effort to cook a soufflé that's as perfect as the one the celebrity chef cooked on TV. She's never satisfied with her effort. Yet, when it comes to getting her to deliver her monthly sales report, she acts as if you're expecting her to write the Great American Novel.

Then you have another employee, a "rock star," who believes that what happens in *his* territory is one hundred percent *his* responsibility. No customer call goes unreturned. No order is too small. He'll drive all night to ensure delivery of what he promised, just to make certain his products are displayed correctly and that the customer is completely satisfied.

So why is this happening? Why is it that some employees have the *"oomph factor"* when it comes to working on something personal, yet when it comes to getting them excited about making lattes, coat hangers, or sales reports, it then becomes a chore...like pulling weeds or cleaning the garage? Why do some employees want to work hard, while others feel like working is just a means to an end?

It's called *discretionary effort*: when an employee puts forward the extra effort because he or she wants to do their job versus feeling they have to do their job.

How do you get your people—your employees—to push themselves, to give one hundred percent or more, in pursuit of success for you and for them? How do you get your employees to give the same one hundred and ten percent to their jobs that they devote to their personal passions? How do you inspire *discretionary effort*?

For too many of today's employees, work is just that—work. It's something to get done so that they can get on to what they really want to do, like socializing, golfing, and cooking.

Since I "up and quit" my job almost two decades ago, I have spent my career counseling some of the world's largest organizations and training their leaders on techniques aimed at getting more out of their employees.

Along that path, I've discovered something different about today's worker. I've found the missing ingredient to the *oomph factor*. In every one, in every business, there beats the heart of a leader, someone who wants to be autonomous, who wants to be his or her own boss—an *Owner*—even if he or she is not a member of the leadership or management team. Even entry-level employees want to make an impact and maximize the fulfillment they find in their jobs.

That's why it's important for all employees, in all kinds of businesses, at every level, to learn that their jobs present them with the opportunity to be *Job Owners*—true leaders of everything they do.

Employees today are looking for something more—a reason to come to work other than just to pick up a paycheck. They need purpose. They want to be emotionally engaged not just in the company, but also in the mission of the company. They need to feel a connection and must buy into the reason you're in business.

They want a chance to become an *Owner*.

I have identified two kinds of employees at any business: *Owners* and *Renters*. An *Owner* naturally gives 110% to the job, because an *Owner* feels the connection to it and its connection to the mission of your company. That connection translates into a sense of responsibility, pride, and satisfaction in his work. Employees who feel these things accept the responsibility to ensure success—their own success, as well as the company's.

Renters think a $25,000-a-year job is a $25,000-a-year job, period. Nothing done within the context of the job description can make the job any more valuable. They take no ownership of any of their actions; because they look upon their jobs as merely fulfilling some menial task, after which they can get back to what is really important to them—their hobbies.

Renters see themselves as simply cogs in the machine. When faced with a question, *Renters* don't make a decision; rather, they slow everything down so that they can seek the answer from someone else, like you. *Renters* never really take responsibility for owning the task or seeking the solution. Asked if there's a better way to do the job, they can't answer; because they feel no sense of pride in improving the job.

Renters are convinced that they're there to "do," not to "think." Work is work only inasmuch as it's what the *Renter* does to earn a living. But if work—the job—is part of a bigger cause, one that's clear and understandable, achievable and *believable*, then work becomes something much more special than a way to finance golf lessons or cooking experiments. It becomes something that, in and of itself, has a goal and purpose behind it. Work then becomes something that an *Owner* will give everything she has to successfully complete.

That's right—an employee can own a job. Not just rent it, but truly own it.

The fact of the matter is that *Owners* are already a rare breed and are becoming more and more scarce. They are on the "endangered list." Yet, you probably have your own stories about *Owners*. Maybe you've always been an *Owner*. Maybe you have someone on your staff who is trying to be an *Owner*. Regardless, the concept of *Job Ownership* isn't a new one. There have always been people who own their jobs—like the employees at Red Bull who decided it would be better to deliver the mail by skateboard. And there have always been leaders who are smart enough to allow the right people to own their jobs, leaders like Tony Hsieh of Zappos! fame.

However, it isn't just the employee who is responsible for taking the leap and asking for more responsibility or taking more initiative. It is actually up to you, the leader, to provide the things *Renters* need to become *Owners*.

For the most part, it's not natural for an employee to feel like he or she can take an authoritative position in any company, especially if those employees are young and new to the organization. The natural mindset of a new hire is one of caution, as he or she gets used to new surroundings and co-workers. But that can't last long; because an employee has to understand that he or she has been brought onboard to add value to the company, not just keep a seat warm.

If you, a member of the company's leadership, see enough in a recruit to hire that person, you see something that brings value to your company. You need to help the new hire by making a few things clear, and then show him how to be an *Owner*.

Yes, it's a new way for everyone in your company to be looking at a "job"; but it's the only way for everyone to look at it if your goal is to have *Job Owners* instead of *Job Renters*.

Part I

RENTERS AND OWNERS

1

OWNERSHIP

OWNING a house or another residence is a pretty straightforward proposition. The bank arranges to lend you money. You take possession of the residence and agree to pay the bank a certain amount in mortgage payments every month for the foreseeable future. Short of the challenges and the crooks that brought us the housing bubble, which burst in 2008, the experience of owning a residence (instead of renting) has been a pretty beneficial concept for all involved. In exchange for the promise to pay the mortgage every month, homeowners have (for the most part) free reign over what the house looks like and how it functions, and are responsible for their own property.

Ironically, homeownership hit the mainstream of American culture at a time when the "company man" was also becoming a fixture in our culture. Home became a castle for the company man. He went to work to improve his life and the lives of his loved ones—a large part of which involved putting a roof over their heads that didn't belong to a landlord. Even in the age of the company man, homeownership brought out the entrepreneur in him, allowing him and his family to become the masters of their surroundings, personalizing their homes on the inside and the outside to reflect their own personalities and their ambitions.

Remember watching movies in your grandparents' media room? Remember the big screen TV...the surround sound... the theater seating? Of course, you don't. It didn't exist. Your grandparents were likely part of the first generation of Americans to own a home, and no one was putting such features in their residences at that time. These houses often consisted of about 1,000 square feet, three bedrooms, and one bathroom, while the family that lived there often consisted of five, six, or seven people. There weren't a lot of secrets in these first owner-occupied houses; but they did allow the people living inside them to be personally invested in keeping these structures in good shape, while improving them whenever they could.

Before World War II, before the company man, most Americans resided in crowded apartment buildings, often called tenements, and had to live by their landlords' rules.

If something went wrong—for instance, a window was broken—the apartment renter had to turn to the landlord for the window to get fixed. If there was insufficient heat in the apartment during the winter, a tenant could insist that the heat be turned up—but only if the rent was increased.

Renters did not have any ownership in anything that could provide them shelter. They didn't have a house they could pass on to loved ones. Renters were at the mercy of a landlord and a lease agreement; once the lease agreement ended, the renter had to find a new place to live or, usually, pay increased rent to stay.

Buildings full of rental apartments routinely became run down, because the people who lived in them day to day didn't care enough about them to keep them up or improve them. Worse, the landlords who owned them didn't have any incentive to keep them from falling apart, either.

For the most part, renters don't (and didn't back then) care much about the property where they reside. They don't care if the mailbox is missing its flag, if the gutters are coming off, or if the doorbell doesn't work. If renters do anything to improve the rental space, it's merely cosmetic and—most importantly—for their own personal benefit, not for the benefit of the home's value. Renters will clean the bathroom, sure; but they aren't going to install a bidet so they can make their rental "roach motel" feel a little more like a Parisian flat.

Today, a house that's owner-occupied is rarely *just* a place to live. A house is now often built or re-designed for "the way we live." As a culture, many of us truly do *own* our homes, even as we're making mortgage payments on them. Home improvement experts like Bob Vila, Norm Abram, Ty Pennington, and others are major celebrities in our culture.

Because we *own* our homes, because our homes are now a part of us and represent who we are, we make them better in every way. That's why homes have continued to markedly improve, decade after decade. In every way, houses have become much better since homeownership became a part of the American Dream. There's more square footage, there are more amenities, and there's more value; often, there's even a media room and enough bathrooms so that no one is waiting outside while Uncle Fred lights a book of matches.

Ownership, too, comes with a built-in incentive for the owner to constantly improve what he or she owns. Renting comes with a built-in incentive to stop improvements once a certain threshold is met, provided any improvements are made at all.

A *job* works the same way as it does with a home.

Think about it. An employee who doesn't own his or her job is doing (with the job) exactly what a renter does with his or her rented residence: *residing in it*, taking up space, making sure nothing changes in it. *Job Renters* do what's needed to get the job done, up to a certain threshold, and no more. The result? *Job Renters* limit the value they bring to the job and the company. Basically, they're there to pick up the proverbial paycheck and go home.

TRUTH GRENADE: If polled, more people in your company or department say they come to work to get paid—nothing more.

Just like homeowners, *Job Owners* give more of themselves, because they know it's their responsibility to improve the job that is theirs. *Owners* show pride in their work, as well as creating more pride in it.

The job isn't just a job for a *Job Owner*. It's an extension of him or her. *Job Owners* have a deep connection to the company and its mission, feeling responsible for their part in achieving that mission in collaboration with their company.

Here's the great thing about creating an organization full of *Job Owners*: even the person occupying the lowest rung on your company's org chart should see his or her job as one that can be owned, that needs to be owned, and that *is* owned.

If you want to grow your company, your division, or your team, you must have *Owners*, not *Renters*. You don't just *hire* these people, you *develop* these people; you don't just *find* them, you *search* for them. You don't just want them, you *need* them; and it's up to you to build an organization of people who can stop thinking like employees and become *Owners*.

2

A WORD TO THE WISE
ABOUT AN ORGANIZATION
FULL OF RENTERS

YOU'LL be looking for a headhunter. Okay, that's six words. But the message is clear: you'll be looking for a headhunter or "executive recruiter" (if you're using a more polite title).

You'll be having employees triumphantly step into your office on a regular basis, putting in their two-week notice. You'll have employees call in sick so often that you'll have the temp agency on speed dial. You'll have employees who are *on their own mission*, trying to do what they believe is right for the company, who realize they don't belong; and they'll eventually leave.

Like me. I know. I did it. I *quit*.

I quit a job that should have turned out to be a career, a lifelong endeavor, a calling. In fact, the company I left had an average stay of thirty-three years per employee. What was I thinking? I was thinking I was an *Owner*, but I was working in a company full of *Renters*, which turned out to be the best thing that ever happened in my professional life.

The company I worked for had "round holes" for jobs and insisted on hiring "round pegs" to fill them. In my mind, one of the great mysteries of the universe—right up there with the origin of the Sphinx—is how I came off during my interview as one of those round pegs. I'm naturally curious. I'm constantly asking questions. My mind races at one hundred miles per hour, and I get excited about the possibilities that any new situation presents. I never accept a new situation as it is. I'm always poking, prodding, learning, and wanting more. I'm like a windup toy with a brain!

Regardless, I was hired; and I really didn't fit in. I kept asking my supervisors questions and was told, "Don't worry about that. Just take care of your job."

I'd come up with a new way of getting something done, and my superiors would insist that I "slow down." I'd need a Cray Supercomputer to tally how many times I was told things like, "There's plenty of time to worry about that later," or "Don't be a maverick. Just stick to the plan."

Plan? What plan? No one ever told me about any *plan*.

My company was lost. It was number three in a field of three. The leaders of the company needed motivation, excitement, new ideas, and fresh blood; but they didn't get it. Why? They didn't have a direction and a clear objective—or if they did, they sure didn't tell *me* about it.

And they sure didn't allow me to use my mind to figure out the best way to help meet the company's objectives. They wanted round pegs to fit into round holes; and I was part octagon, part narrow ellipse. How was I ever going to fit in?

The frustrating part (in spite of the fact that I kept trying to improve what I was doing) was that my company received just enough value from me to keep me employed, while giving me the occasional raise. So in reality, I was receiving mixed signals everywhere, all the time.

I recall getting a promotion where my new responsibility was to lead a team of people who worked in different cities around the country, each in a different market. This group was sort of a forgotten army that brought very little to the company's bottom line. My plan was to grow this division and see if the company could realize its potential.

The person who'd led this team before me gave lifeless direction and was more of a glorified administrator than anything else. So I thought affecting change would be easy. I jumped in with both feet and very little direction from my superior.

Immediately, I took *Ownership* of the position. I started implementing my ideas and brought a much-needed feeling of unity to the group. I wrote a mission for the team, defined job descriptions for each member, met one-on-one, put together weeklong training programs, and even had a logo made for the group to help make everyone feel included, like they were a part of an important mission.

The team was ecstatic! Finally, someone was getting them the resources, training, and direction they needed to effectively do their jobs. Ideas were implemented. Everyone had a place. Everyone understood his or her role. Before long, we were moving the needle and driving results for the company, until...

"DAHLSTROM! STOP, YOU MAVERICK. WHAT ARE YOU DOING? JUST DO WHAT YOU'RE TOLD TO DO."

That insightful piece of leadership advice came from my boss. It was three months after I'd been promoted to take over this previously underperforming team. I had put practices in place that were already showing positive results, and now I was being told that I was not doing it right.

"Just do what you're told? What does that mean?" I asked my superior. "Does that mean leading the team the same lethargic, apathetic way it's been led for years?"

Politically, that was probably not the right thing to say. But I did get my point across.

Anyone can tell you that business-building activities are better for everyone. And what builds business better than incremental sales? But a member of leadership who's insecure about his department, his turf, his "property," and his hires is naturally going to treat those hires like they're invading his professional domicile. The result is that the boss continues doing what comes naturally to someone who's insecure in his position of authority: he'll show everyone who's boss by using some classic fear tactic or rear-view management.

My boss was so focused on *how* things were done—and if they were being done *the way he'd like them to be done*—that he found no satisfaction in the positive results.

I'd been given a responsibility, and I'd taken that responsibility seriously. But my boss, apparently, didn't expect me to take that responsibility to heart and act on it the way I did. Basically, after I was told to stop everything I was implementing, I was told to perform my new job *exactly the same way* it had been performed before I took the position. Translation? Poorly.

I didn't want to do my work poorly. I didn't want to just go through the motions. I didn't want my office to be just a place where I mentally punched a clock and spent the next eight hours. I could do that with a cell phone and a toilet stall.

My business card stood for something greater than just the place where I worked; it was a part of who I was and the professional life I wanted to build for myself. I didn't shut down my thoughts about work when I left for the evening, when I was out with friends or co-workers, when I was running errands, or when I was sitting in my apartment at night. I was constantly thinking about ways to improve the parts of the business I touched that would, in turn, touch me.

However, I was constantly being frustrated when I tried to implement my thinking or take advantage of my strengths. I was often told I was a "maverick" and that I didn't follow the company's procedures. What procedures? No one ever told me about any procedures, written or otherwise. For that matter, I really had no idea what the company wanted to do or where I fit in the company's bigger plan. All I knew was that we were number three in our industry, and I was trying to make us number one...plain and simple.

Well, a few weeks later, I decided I'd had enough. The communication was awful, as was the culture—as was my feeling about the whole place. Unfortunately, I was turning into a terrible employee; and there was no way I was going to be a good one in a culture like that. The ludicrous part was that my attitude couldn't have been better; all I wanted to do was improve the company that employed me. But I never felt like I had the freedom to take responsibility for my own actions and ideas.

In reviewing my years with the company, I realized that I never really fit in.

I thought about the people I'd known at work who were doing less than I had done, who were taking on less responsibility, but who were still moving higher and higher up the company ladder. I realized that they were better than I was at only one simple, albeit vital, business skill— kissing ass. In meetings, at lunches, at company retreats, I wasn't really "on the team"; because I wanted more than to kiss ass. I was discussing business-forwarding ideas, instead of scouting out the proverbial tush to tickle or sitting in on what I called the "Pods of The Pissed-Off."

You know them...the louses who are so unhappy with their jobs that they're on the lookout for other pissed-off folks who are itching to bitch about the company.

After quitting, I returned to my apartment feeling more frustrated than upset. Frustration trumped my worry about how I'd pay my bills. Frustration was the overriding emotion I felt at the time; oddly, it was the same frustration I'd felt about my job. But this frustration was even more intense now that I didn't hold that job anymore. I couldn't entirely put my finger on why I was so frustrated, why I kept shaking my head, pursing my lips, and using the full vocabulary of colorful words I'd learned when I was a kid sitting next to my dad at Boston Red Sox games.

The frustration lingered. So I quoted Dad...often.

Then, a few days later, it came to me. It came to me as I sat in the living room of my apartment—my *rented* apartment—my rented apartment with its stark white walls, flimsy folding closet doors, worn-down carpet, and cheap Formica® countertops. My rented apartment with the shower drain that worked twenty-four hours a day— because it took twenty-four hours to fully drain the tub from my morning shower.

I remembered a few years earlier, when I'd first walked in and saw 600 square feet of "blah," that I thoroughly convinced myself I could make it my own, that I could be the *Owner* of this apartment, this space. I'd done a few things to make the place look better, like putting some pictures on the walls. I also set out my personal collection of Italian pasta jars on the counter next to the stove—the stove whose only working burner took thirty minutes to bring water to a boil.

I looked around. The stuff was mine, but the place wasn't. I was just holding down the fort for someone else, keeping it "weatherized" for the building's owner and remotely habitable for the next person who was going to rent it. I had been writing rent checks month after month, but my place and living situation never really got any better. Eventually, when my lease was up, I would have to leave this apartment as stark white and "blah" as I'd found it. Every hole I'd pounded into the walls to hang photos of family members, friends, and places I'd been would have to be filled with spackle and sanded smooth, just to give myself the remote possibility of getting my security deposit back.

Sure, I could just fill those holes with toothpaste, but I quickly realized that I only had a tube of bright blue Colgate® gel in the bathroom. That made me start using some of those words Dad taught me again. This was (long) *before* the Red Sox ended their eighty-six-year World Series famine.

It was right then, right there, and in "mid-profanity" that I realized why my frustration with my "lost" calling overpowered any possible worry over what was next. It came to me then that my apartment was just like the job from which I had left. I'd left the job the same way I'd found it when I'd been promoted a few months earlier...no better, no worse. My former company would have to fill the position again with someone who they hoped would be the "round peg" they were looking for to fit their "round hole." It hadn't been my job at all. It was someone else's job that I was renting.

That was it! I was *renting* something that I wanted to *own*. I hadn't been allowed to make the job any better than it had been the day I "assumed the position." I realized I couldn't think like a mere employee. They wanted a *Renter*. I needed to be an *Owner*.

By coming to that realization, I changed my professional life forever. I made a promise to myself that I would always *own* my job in the future...and only work for a company that wanted *Owners*. I would own the time I spent working on the job, thinking about the job, and executing the job. I would make sure that I made the job better and, therefore, make myself better every day that I worked at it. I wasn't at all worried about being unemployed at that moment; because I knew that I was going to find the right fit for me soon enough, a fit that would allow me to be the *Owner* of what I did for a living.

Then I took stock of my surroundings and made another decision: to go to the store and get a tube of stark white toothpaste.

TRUTH GRENADE: *Owners* **are the ones who want to make a dent in the universe. The problem is, they just don't know how. You've probably got an army full of** *Owners* **and have never given them what they need: the chance at** *Ownership.*

3

TODAY'S EMPLOYEE

THE simple truth is, today's workforce is mobile, the economy is ultra-dynamic, and the list of jobs and great places to work are changing year over year. Twenty or thirty years ago, the job of "Website Designer" didn't exist. Therefore, no one could live in a Rocky Mountain ski town working as a website designer at night for clients in New York, London, Macau, and Durham, North Carolina, so that they could ski all day. But today's economy is full of such businesses and people, and what I call "Gen-preneurs," the newest evolution of the do-it-yourselfer who sees opportunity around every corner, including the short stay he or she had (or is having) at your company.

The people who fill these positions "work to live," rather than "live to work." More than any earlier generation, today's employees know that experiences matter more than anything else; and they're looking for good work experiences, as well as good life experiences. With so many unique ways for people to earn a living today, experiences can be interchangeable for today's workers, meaning that work really can, and should be, a passion... an experience.

They saw their grandparents toil at GM doing the same (often dangerous and dreadful) job for thirty years and living in the same house since the day they took the job. Then their grandparents retired the day they paid off the mortgage; and now they spend six months a year in Florida with their friends, Bea and Ned, all of who live on their pensions.

Even the parents of today's younger employees—many of them Boomers and some a little younger—faced entirely different challenges. Tough times in the '70s and early '80s caused uncertainty at work and instability at home. Breadwinners jumped from one job to another, from one industry to another. Sometimes the job-hopping was for the better; sometimes it was for the worse. But the fact remained that the American workplace was evolving away from the job-for-life proposition that it was during the era of the company man.

In just two generations, the American workforce has become an entirely different animal. Employees now are almost like free agents bouncing from job to job.

I know a guy who's an art buyer at an advertising agency. Five years ago, he was a private investigator for an insurance company. "What are the related disciplines?" I asked him.

"A lot of legalities involved in both," he reported. "I put my law degree to work constantly in both jobs."

Who knew?

The point is that no one is on the same work treadmill, chained to an unsatisfying job, forced to work for a leader or company that doesn't match the worker's ethics, values, needs, or wants. Now people simply leave a job if every morning feels like *Groundhog Day*. So why should an employee make the effort to *own* a job? And why would an employer *want* an employee to *own* a job?

Some of the best organizations in the world, many in business for generations, are now seeing a new kind of worker come through the door. This new kind of employee wants nothing to do with how his or her grandparents (or even parents) lived their lives. He or she doesn't want to commit to a single company and then be kicked to the proverbial curb after years of productive service, days before retirement, and heartbreakingly short of receiving a full pension. This new worker wants to take his destiny into his own hands.

However confident the exterior, fear runs through the tender newbie-worker. This new generation has debt—*huge* student debt. This fact, balanced with their need for experience, not just a job, shakes their confidence. Their present workplace resembles, to them, a game of chicken; will the employer let them go—or be forced to let them go—before they're able to secure their next job? That's the attitude many of today's employees are bringing to work. Their present jobs are simply a stopover on their Worldwide Job Tour, where they can loot a company for the lessons and treasures that they can take to their next work experience with the hope of making more money—to pay off that student debt!

Another challenge you will have with these tech-savvy Gen-preneurs is the way they think about the way you do business. To them, it's slow and outdated. Chances are, it is. Again, think about the personality of this generation; these people have never known life without a computer, and many of them have never known life without the Internet.

A computer's main purpose is automating repeatable activities, which improves efficiency. In many ways, these young employees *are* computers. They think of things in terms of efficiency. Their brains are wired to look at just about any task and find the tool to help them do it smarter, faster, and more efficiently. Why else do you read about all these young people developing apps for this and apps for that? Their purpose is to make life and work more efficient (and interesting), so they can get done with their jobs and get on to what is more fun for them. If you understand what motivates today's young worker, you will take advantage of, and benefit from, the younger worker's wisdom.

How do you look at your company? Do you look at it as just a place where people can park themselves and make themselves more valuable for someone else? Of course not! You are fertile ground for the up-and-coming next generation of *Owners* who want more—and it's your company that will give them the security and freedom for which they're looking. Yours is a company that will turn *Renters* into landowners and tenants into proprietors...a company that will get its employees to stop thinking like employees and more like *Owners*.

4

DISCRETIONARY EFFORT

DISCRETIONARY Effort: that little something extra that a person gives to a project, job, or venture when he decides he wants to do it versus when he feels he has to do it.

Author Brady G. Wilson writes about discretionary effort in *Love at Work: Why Passion Drives Performance in the Feelings Economy*. Leslie Wilk Braksick, Ph.D., also has plenty to say about discretionary effort in *Unlock Behavior, Unleash Profits: Developing Leadership Behavior That Drives Profitability in Your Organization*. This discretionary effort is the one hundred and ten percent that you see in some of your employees—your *Owners*. According to Dr. Braksick, it is "...the extra level of performance people give when they want to do something as opposed to when they feel like they have to do something."

I call it the *"oomph factor"*...giving that something extra required, because you know it's the right thing. It is just like when someone feels that she owns her own business—an *Owner*, for real.

There are a myriad of reasons why people start businesses, and one of the most common is that they believe they can do it better than anyone else. So it's never, "I want to run a business;" it's..."I know I can do it better. I know there's a need."

A kid named Joey started the most impressive business I've run across recently. Joey is the 20-something who runs the concession stand during the summer months at my neighborhood pool. A catering company that's located about thirty miles from my house employs Joey. He lives with three other guys his age in a loft in downtown Denver, which is about twenty miles from where I live. So how do I know Joey so well? And how can he run his business if he's already employed by a catering company?

Well, it turns out that Joey was one of the most *Owner-*like *employees* I've met in some time. So much so, that he made it into this book and into just about every speech I give. *I owe Joey a lot.*

The catering company for which Joey works owns the concession stand at the pool in my neighborhood. Every summer they send someone to tend to the stand, selling swimmers ice cream cones and soft drinks from a cooler.

In reality, the concession stand was nothing more than a glorified poolside table with a sign.

The summer that Joey took over the concession stand, many things changed. First off, a cart had replaced the table. Secondly, there were numerous new items available, including hot pretzels, hot dogs, and ice cream sandwiches. Third, the concession stand actually did business.

At the beginning of the summer, I was at the pool when I stepped up to the new cart and ordered a Pepsi. Right after I placed my order, I opened my wallet and realized I didn't have any cash. I quickly reneged on my order, told Joey I'd come back later when I had money, and started heading back to my poolside seat.

"You don't need cash this summer," Joey spoke up. I sarcastically asked if he was giving refreshments away. He told me that he had set up a merchant account for the concession stand, so that people in the neighborhood could sign for their orders; and the charge would appear on their credit card bills monthly. "No one wants to bring cash or credit cards to the pool," he said in a confident fashion. It was like he'd run focus groups all winter.

I opened an account with him and found myself spending much more at the pool that summer than I ever had before.

Of course, I also enjoyed myself a lot more than ever before. Instead of some aloof kid sitting at the table reading *People* magazine and digging stuff out of an under-stocked cooler whenever someone ordered something, our pool now had a person who was really engaged in what he was doing. As the summer went on, I got to know Joey well. We talked business a lot, and I loved some of his initiatives. He offered ice cream sandwiches for the kids, fountain drinks, and hot dogs and brats with fresh onions and pickles. People beat a path to the concession stand.

Even though his shift was to go from 10 a.m. to 6 p.m., Joey stayed late on Fridays and started "Grill Night." He would grill burgers, chicken wings, and even ribs. It was a wonderful way to end the week and allowed this guy, this twenty-five-year-old kid, to really become a part of the neighborhood's fabric. "Grill Night" was usually finished by 8:00 p.m., as many of us would adjourn to a neighbor's house for beer or a glass of wine.

On one of the last Fridays of the summer, I was standing talking to Joey and mentioned it would be great to have a beer here, at the pool, instead of heading to our house or a neighbor's. At the moment, I really didn't think much of it. It was a simple conversation, off the cuff. But nothing a customer suggested was off the cuff to Joey.

The last weekend of operation for our neighborhood pool is always Labor Day weekend. With it comes the closing of our neighborhood social gatherings and, of course, the concession cart Joey had manned all summer. Talking with Joey that weekend, I wrapped up my summer exploration of his entrepreneurial valor. I asked him if he thought that he had made more money this summer now that the concession stand bought this cart for him to use.

"Well, actually, all the catering company wanted me to do was pick up sodas and stuff at the store, put it in the cooler, and sell it during the week here. But in the spring, I saw how many people came to the pool—even before it got hot; so I asked my company to invest in a better cart," he explained. "They turned me down. They said they didn't want to invest any more money up here '...because the *Owners* here spend very little.' So I bought the cart myself."

"Wow," I thought, "what a kid." Then I asked, "How long did it take you to pay off the cart?"

"By the end of the first week I was here," he responded.

I almost spit out my Pepsi.

A simple idea like turning a concession table into a true concession stand had made a huge difference in the sales during the summer.

We spoke for a while more before Joey asked me about the "Clubhouse," a new building that had gone up near the pool. The Clubhouse was built to be a multi-purpose building where people in the neighborhood can host big parties or meetings. There are a few rooms in there, including a "theater room" that people can use to watch their DVDs, nice furniture, a deck that looks out at the mountains, a full kitchen, and one other feature that had piqued Joey's interest.

"What's the deal with the bar area in there?" he asked.

I told him that the people hosting parties could use the bar and hire a bartender. There are glasses for any kind of drink, an icemaker, a refrigerator, and even a dishwasher. "Of course," I told him, "people have to furnish their own liquor."

I could see the proverbial gears turning in Joey's head and wasn't the least bit surprised to learn a couple weeks later that he'd made another proposal to his catering company. This one was to open the bar at the Clubhouse every Friday night, as well as Saturday and Sunday, during the winter.

Once he got the initial approval from the catering company, Joey had to get buy-in from our homeowners association. *This was not a hard sell.* The neighbors who sit on the board jumped for joy when they heard the idea of opening an area of our new clubhouse to offer residents drinks and cocktails on the weekends. "What an idea!" I heard them all say some time later.

Next, Joey set out about the business of securing a liquor license. This was not as easy as getting the fermented board members to approve their piece of the plan. Part of the requirement (above the necessary $2,500) was to gather 250 signatures from residents, both inside and outside our neighborhood.

Late on an autumn Saturday afternoon, a few weeks after Joey's summer stint at the pool had ended, the doorbell rang. I opened the door; and there stood Joey, clipboard in hand, smile on his face, and a pitch to sell. There stood the kid to whom I had mentioned, only briefly, on a hot summer's day, that I didn't have cash for a Pepsi...while being forced to watch children playing in the pool and listen to the neighbors talk about who was driving what, what new curtains the Klinger's had in the front windows, or what school Braden was attending next year. He had a solution for that; and, all the while, Joey was executing his overall plan.

Now, as summer was turning to fall, he was standing at my front door asking me for the fifty-fourth signature on his quest for 250. Joey had an idea. He took *ownership*. He saw the upside and decided that it was his mission to accommodate a bunch of fat guys in this planned community in South Denver. He found his mission, knew the outcome he wanted to achieve, and set out to accomplish the task. This is something he *wanted* to do, not something he *had* to do.

Bringing some *ownership thinking* to a job that others have treated as little more than a mundane task, like selling concessions by the pool, represents the *ownership* thinking everyone should want in his company.

Truth Grenade: 99.99% of you are afraid to employ someone like Joey; 99.99% should employ lots of people like Joey.

Joey brought initiative that far too many employees don't have or are discouraged from putting on display to their employers. I have no idea what Joey was earning when he first arrived at the neighborhood pool, but he made the job of serving our neighborhood much more valuable once he took some true initiative.

When people believe in the mission at hand *and* have the tools and room to succeed, they become *Owners*. The discretionary effort put forth creates extraordinary things. It delivers results, changes thinking, solves problems, and feeds on itself, which positively reinforces further extra effort. Across the board, when a person sees the benefit in his or her effort, and they feel they are helping achieve something greater and something bigger, that person is much more likely to develop a "want-to-do" attitude versus a "have-to-do" attitude. *That's discretionary effort.*

5

CHANGING BEHAVIOR

THE key benefit to building an organization of *Owners* is how things change around your place of business—specifically, people's behaviors. When people have bought into what you're trying to accomplish, know exactly what is expected of them, and understand they'll be held accountable for the results, their decision-making process changes, and with it, so does their behavior. Suddenly people's actions shift, consciously or subconsciously, in a single direction that creates waves of success that would otherwise not be seen in the organization.

Case in point...Bubba's Burgers, the old-fashioned, authentically served hamburger joint in Hawaii that's been feeding surfers and tourists since 1936. If you've never had a Double Bubba, you can easily imagine what one would taste like. It's the way a burger should be served: cooked on a griddle, with a toasted bun, mustard, old-fashioned ketchup, relish, and diced onions. Heck, Bubba's doesn't even want lettuce and tomato on the burger, fearful that they may take away from the authenticity of the burger. The burgers aren't just a meal; they are truly an experience.

Imagine, if you will, a Bubba Burger joint with its simplistic walk-up outdoor counter, two employees, self-serve water, and primarily outdoor seating where you can enjoy your burger.

There are only two employees who run the entire joint— usually young girls wearing cut-off jean shorts, bikini tops, and a smile. They take orders, collect money, cook the burgers, fries, and onion rings, and then joust with the occasional tourist who complains that the place is covered in Red Sox paraphernalia.

At a recent visit to Bubba's, we were treated to the type of *ownership thinking* employers should grant their employees.

Certainly Bubba's wouldn't turn away any local interested in consuming one of its magnificent burgers. But Bubba's mainly wants the tourist dollar.

As tourists, my family and I waited with great anticipation for our forthcoming lunch. We were seated outside next to

Al, a retiree from New York, with lots of stories to tell two little blonde boys interested in listening.

After a quick five minutes, our lunch arrived. Al, now looking at the burgers we had ordered, realized he'd ordered himself a Double Bubba the recommended way... without lettuce or tomato.

No big deal, right? Not for Al. Al quickly reverted back to his New York ways, verbalizing his disappointment about his impending meal. During his rant about how he'd ordered it the way Bubba intended it, his burger arrived.

At this point, the two young ladies working the burger stand were fully aware of Al's disappointment. Again, you might say, no big deal, right? Just get the bellowing guy a side of lettuce and tomato, right?

Without hesitation, one of the young ladies left Al's lunch at his table without saying a word. Al, with the slightest bit of sarcasm in his voice, leaned over towards me and said, "It's because she hates the Yankees!" Before he was finished saying the word "Yankees," the young woman was back—with another hamburger. This one, compliments of Bubba, included both lettuce and tomato.

"I thought the Double Bubba was only one burger," said Al.

"It is," replied the waitress. "This one is on the house and is how you said you wanted it originally. Enjoy."

After completing our meal, I stopped up at the checkout to have a quick word with the waitress. She explained the delivery of the second burger to Al by simply pointing to the sign on the wall, which read: *We cheat tourists, drunks, and attorneys*. Then she said, "It's really not true. Our job is to make everyone happy."

And with that, it dawned on me that Bubba is one smart dude. He's clearly an employer who believes in the value of giving his employees the autonomy to succeed and the trust to make the right decisions. By doing that, behavior will change.

TRUTH GRENADE: If the people who work for you aren't performing, it is simply because you haven't given them a reason for changing their behavior—you haven't sold them on why they need to give more of themselves.

When people believe that their ten-, twelve-, or fourteen-hour workdays have meaning, they begin to understand that their hard work will pay off in the end...that they'll be a part of accomplishing something bigger. They will make decisions in a way that benefits the organization, all the while helping achieve the defined *Goal*.

Behavior changes when your employees understand how they are a vital part of the success of the organization. Sure, you need to define boundaries for people; but once they believe in the mission (the *Goal*), they will make decisions that move the company towards that end. This is the power of changing behaviors—making better decisions that benefit the company.

6

FINDING OWNERS

RENTERS and *Owners*...you've had both. You *have* both. The question is: How do you find more *Owners*?

I would hope it's safe to say at this point, since you're reading this book, that you *would like* a team entirely full of *Owners*. But the fact of the matter is, you probably have too many *Renters*.

So what makes someone an Owner and another person a Renter?

Why do some employees give you everything they've got, while others seem to give you nothing but grief? Why do some employees solve problems, while other employees are human problem multipliers? Why do some people come to work with the positive attitude that *this job is my job to improve*, that everything around them somehow represents their calling, their mission?

Many employers think it's entirely up to the employee, that, "You never really know what you've got until the new hire gets into the job." Right? That's what we call a crapshoot—a roll of the dice, "black or red."

One thing I can't impress upon you enough is that this whole process is anything but a crapshoot. You also might say the trick is to ensure that you, the employer, make the *extra* effort during the interviewing process to hire people who are going to be good employees, employees who will accept the responsibilities of the job, and perform them well. You want people who, during their interviews, say something more than what they want their salaries to be and inquire as to how many weeks of vacation they'll get.

Good luck with that.

Don't you already make the *extra* effort to hire the best people? Of course, you do. No employer goes into the interview process thinking:

"I'm looking for the laziest waste of oxygen I can possibly find to fill this position. And then I'm going to worry about that person's performance every day, spend time asking others to 'cover' for that employee, and finally, cut that employee a big severance check before I start interviewing once again to fill that position."

Nope, employers look at an open position as something to be filled by a capable person who can solve the problems that come across his or her desk. An employee who solves problems means that others in the workplace can concentrate on their own responsibilities, and then the workplace can hum like a finely-tuned Swiss watch.

But you don't just hire *Owners*. You hire employees; and then you turn those employees into *Owners*, by giving them what they need so they *want* to do more. You develop them into something more than just people who *rent* their jobs. The simple fact is that your ability to have a staff full of happy, satisfied, productive employees has more to do with *you* than with the person you're interviewing.

A company that has *Owners* has more than employees. A company with a staff full of *Owners* has "business-forwarders," people who take it upon themselves to be accountable to their company, their co-workers, and themselves at the same time. They look at what they do for their company as something they do for themselves. They share the company's plans and make decisions every day that bring those plans to life.

The way *Owners* feel about their jobs—the pride and determination that they bring to performing their duties—

is a product of the environment in which they work and *what you provide for them*. Yep, you! Stop looking over your shoulder for someone to help.

Everyone knows a job is not like, say, a cell phone. You can own a cell phone simply by paying for it. A job's not a bag of groceries or a new shirt. You don't just buy it and, thereby, own it. So is it possible that someone can really *own* a job?

"Of course someone can own his job," you may be saying to yourself. *"I own my job."*

As a matter of fact, if you're a member of the leadership team, you may indeed believe that you own the jobs of the people who work for you. For that matter, you may feel like you own the jobs of the people who work under the people who work for you. You may even think you own the job of the kid who's taken the relatively lowly position of mailroom clerk. You own all of their jobs, right? They are, after all, *your* employees.

That's the sort of control a *Job Owner* has, isn't it? That has to be the mentality of someone who takes on the responsibilities of management, the sort of heavy authority a *Job Owner* has, right? Right?

Wrong! So wrong! Completely wrong!

You own *your* job. And everyone who works for you, even the kid who just started in the mailroom, owns *his* job, too. At least they should.

If they don't, you need to help them do so—now!

But how? You see your employees every day. They know you're watching them do their jobs. So they have to take charge of them, right? They have to own it. They can't just rent their jobs when you're there hovering over them, right?

Wrong once again, Charlie. Employees are a lot like apartment renters. Their natural mentality is that, *"I just rent this place. I don't own it. Why should I try to make it any better?"*

And *Job Renters* only take action when absolutely necessary—or when you, as management, tell them to take action. Right? How often do you find yourself giving direction after direction to your employees about stuff they really should know? How often does your phone ring with another employee asking for your opinion, waiting for you to give them instruction?

Your employees look upon themselves as simply corporate appendages of you in the executive suite—doing things that you would do if you weren't so busy in your big office getting a manicure, exercising stock options, and ordering your secretary to make dinner reservations for you and your wife. *That's the way Job Renters think.*

They have no connection to what you or the company is trying to accomplish. They don't recognize what you, in leadership, do to push the business forward. So they don't know where their jobs fit within the company's mission. And I'm afraid to tell you this, but the more you hover over them and micromanage their day today, the more you will have to hover over them and micromanage their day tomorrow.

TRUTH GRENADE: The more you do your employees' work, the more you will have to do your employees' work.

There is a formula for making sure that you can build the organization or department you want; and it starts with assembling the right staff of people who you believe can initiate solutions and who, if given the right tools, will deliver above and beyond your expectations. They're called

Owners. Your job is to find them or turn those already in your company into *Owners*. Whether they were that way when you hired them or you implement the kind of change required to develop the right culture, your business will run more smoothly than you ever imagined.

So...do you want *Owners* or do you want *Renters*?

7

NEEDS

HERE'S how it goes. Everyone, including—and especially—your employees, has needs. It's up to you to fulfill those needs. You might ask, "What more could they possibly need? I give them everything."

A job description, a security card, a comfortable chair and desk, and free coffee every morning—that isn't "everything."

In fact, it's barely anything. Unlimited cell phone minutes and a company car...sure, those are nice; and they're absolutely necessary for some employees to perform their jobs. But, again, that's barely anything if you're looking to get the best out of your employees.

For years I've worked with organizations that expect their employees to come to work every day and improve results from the prior week, prior month, and prior year.

From salespeople to administrators to senior leaders, the challenge has always been the attitude of, "That was nice, but that was yesterday. What have you done for me today? What will you do now?"

As a successful leader, your job is to build an organization of people who *want* to work harder, who feel a sense of pride and satisfaction with their jobs, and want the company to win. In fact, it's more important now than ever before because the company man no longer exists.

Getting people to stop thinking like employees is about getting them to want to stay and want to give more, constantly adding value to your organization. It's not just about being a part of your organization, but becoming a part of what your organization is. Even though your staff is full of employees, they can still participate in dictating what your organization is all about...if they *own* their jobs. A great friend of mine used to say, "You define your company's culture, not the other way around."

You see, employees have needs. I'm talking about more than the training required to recite the welcome slogan when a customer approaches one of your baristas: *"Hi, welcome to Cam's Coffee Cave! Would you like to try one of our new frozen head-freezes?"*

To keep Gen-preneurs, for that matter, any employee, invested in your business, you need to provide them with some simple things.

First, you need to let them know why you're there. Not you specifically, but why your company does what it does.

"Why?" you might ask.

Why do they need to know why your company does what it does? Ask author Simon Sinek, who wrote the truth-telling book *Start with Why: How Great Leaders Inspire Everyone to Take Action*. Sinek's position is that if you start by defining the *Why*, people will be inspired to achieve remarkable things.

The notion that people can rally behind the *Why* does, in fact, compel people to achieve more. Let me explain:

Your employees come to work, some of them for fifty hours a week or more. But for what—a paycheck? They need a purpose in their work. And more than any other generation, today they need to understand your purpose, your *Why*. A paycheck is little more than a byproduct. It alone does not give them purpose.

Many of today's generation of employees are so goal-oriented that, without a goal, they become aimless and bored very easily. A goal gives them something that nothing else in their lives can; it gives them inclusion, connection, and association. *They love to be loved.* That's part of their make-up. They have been coddled even before exiting the womb, a trophy at every position, and a medal just for finishing the race. Defining your company's *Why* provides employees with the added benefit of why they should come to work and do a superb job. They need to know that what they're doing is adding up to something... an end result.

TRUTH GRENADE: Chances are you know your company's *Why*. Chances are 99% of your employees don't.

Secondly, they need to know that *What* they do at work moves the company toward the *Why*. That means defining for them exactly what their roles are, how those roles are connected to the company's overall purpose, then training them to perform those roles with purpose. Again, such an action gives them the feeling that their efforts—and even their existence—are important to the well-being of something much bigger, that they are the gasoline that's fueling the engine that is moving the company forward toward its *Goal*.

If you think about your most recent workforce employees, you'll recall that they're probably well-educated. In fact, the people entering the workforce now are the most educated generation in our country's history, even more than the carefree Gen-Xer. With all of this education comes expectations. From this generation's standpoint, this education should bring with it more opportunities.

For the past twenty to twenty-five years, the conversation at your youngest employee's dinner table with his or her parents has sounded something like this: "If you go to school, work hard, and finish college, you can have any job you want and rise to any position you seek."

That message has been pounded into their heads over and over, creating a level of expectation that might be a little hard for you to fulfill as the employer. That's because they may now be saying to themselves, *"Hey, I've gotten my degree; and I've been here ninety days already. How come I'm not a VP yet?"*

Like waves are to an ocean, training for these employees is also assumed. I've been hiring college kids for years for various intern positions—mail runner to lunch runner. My business runs on youth. When I interview my next great employee, I have only one request—*bring your favorite book to the interview*. Sounds simple, right? You would be surprised what the conversation sounds like from my side of the table at Starbucks: "I didn't know what you meant by 'bring your favorite book.'"

Those interviewees don't even get a free cup of coffee. For those who do make it past my entrance exam and show up with a cookbook, a history book, or a book on Tai Chi, the conversation goes much better.

After finding out about their interests, likes, and dislikes, the conversation always, *always* turns to...training...as in how much will they get, when will they be trained, and do I have any formal training systems. To our youth, training is seen as part of the gig, a common denominator for anyone applying for a new job. This simple fact separates the present generation of worker from the last.

Most of us learned what we needed to know on the job—thrown to the wolves, if you will. Training was doing. I once met a bicycle sales rep who was told on his first day to, "Drive down Route 1 until you see a bike on the top of an old barn. Stop there, and meet Jimmy. Get his order;

and once you're done, ask Jimmy how to get to Kevin's. He'll give you directions. We'll see you back here at five."

That was training then.

Today, your employees expect much, much more. This educated, up-and-coming group won't have the personal intellect to take any matter into their own hands. They have almost no street smarts. They have literally been told what to do, when to do it, and what the result should be since the time they were in diapers. This kind of upbringing leads to *needs*.

Giving your employees what they need isn't really complicated. Outside the details of their jobs—how to do them, when to do them, and the expected results—they need to feel included. They need to be involved. They need more than just direction—how to do their jobs; they need to know *why* they perform their jobs. Giving today's employees what they need includes more than just tools. It includes telling them that you expect them to be involved in the company's *Why*. Their role is critical to the success of your organization; without your employees, you simply won't succeed.

Lastly, employees need trust...trust that you've hired the right person for the job and that they will do the job you hired them to do. We're all short on trust these days. Too many managers micromanage; you're too worried about the process—not the outcome. Today's workers need your trust to show them that you have confidence in them. We simply don't give enough trust. Why? Leaders are too afraid of the consequences...the consequences that come from hiring the wrong person or not giving them what they *need*.

Give employees what they need and, chances are, you'll be on the receiving end of the results from some extremely smart, overachieving *Job Owners*.

8

OWNERSHIP STARTS WITH YOU

SO...do you want to build an organization full of *Job Owners*? Do you want your employees to feel confident enough to think they do, indeed, own their jobs? Think about it: not everyone is especially entrepreneurial, after all. Many of your employees have probably only been employees—as opposed to entrepreneurs—for the simple reason that they aren't entrepreneurial. So, can employees who aren't entrepreneurial really *own* their jobs?

Actually, owning a job has nothing to do with being an entrepreneur. It has everything to do with the message sent by leadership.

Leadership's job is to deliver results. Delivering good results, however, is largely incumbent upon the people who work *under* leadership. These are the people who do the "dirty work," the "grunt work," the "everyday jobs" that contribute so greatly to the company's results. People who do these jobs don't always see how their jobs contribute to the results, and that's a problem no matter what industry you're in.

It's up to leadership to make sure employees understand how their jobs contribute to the company's results. Only then will the people who perform those jobs do so in the best possible way.

Why hire people and then waste time micro-managing them to the point where they're nothing more than automatons? And how much time is wasted looking over the shoulder of these people, time that could be used in business-building enterprises?

Whether you've thought about it this way or not, your job as a leader is to develop people who become proficient enough that they can replace you tomorrow. Chipotle, the fabulously successful restaurant chain, has an impressive promote-from-within policy that keeps employees with the company for years on end. However, no Chipotle employee can be promoted unless, and until, that employee has actually trained a replacement to take the job he or she is vacating.

Bad leaders find that sort of policy a setup for their own demise. Good leaders view the policy as a great way to expand the ability of the company's workforce. They also look at it as a way to free the people moving up in the organization to look for more opportunities to develop the business in new markets and in new ways.

When you begin to help your people become better at what they do, you will quickly know who are *Owners* and who are *Renters* by their engagement...or lack thereof.

Ownership thinking starts with you! Do you trust the people who work for you? Do you hover over your employees, micromanaging their decisions because you don't believe they will make the right ones? Are you teaching them what you know about the job, helping them become better at what they do, or do you just expect they will improve by themselves, just as you did? Are you asking your employees what they think are solutions to problems, or are you simply giving them the answers? Could your team, without hesitation, recite your company's mission? If so, do they believe this mission is worthwhile and important? If so, do they understand the importance of their jobs within the mission?

Are you a coach or just a manager?

TRUTH GRENADE: Most managers are really just landlords, suspiciously keeping an eye on their property—never trusting the employee to successfully complete what they were hired to do in the first place.

Part II:

GOALS, ROLES, AND ROPE

GOALS

9

GOALS

WALTER S. Mack was a New York businessman who, in 1938, took over a scrappy little company that was trying to compete with a giant. Mack was up against a big competitor in Atlanta, which had all the advantages in what passed for the cola wars in that era.

In 1939, a year after Mack took over Pepsi, his company's $5 million in annual sales was dwarfed by Coke's $128 million.[1] So Mack had to do some out-of-the-box thinking in order for his company simply to survive, much less thrive. He decided to hire a special sales team to help make Pepsi available in previously untapped markets all over the country.

The challenge for Mack's new team was that there was no roadmap for making headway into these untapped markets at that time. There were no books or marketing consultants to guide them. But that didn't stop them.

---

1 nytimes.com/2007/02/04/books/review/Goldstein.t.html

"I knew what we needed to do," said one of the salesmen who Mack hired shortly after the Special Markets department was assembled.[2] It was clear to everyone in this new sales force what their charge was, and it was up to them to get the job done. The members of the sales team would have to be industrious. They'd have to find new ways to market a fairly mainstream, though not particularly popular, American brand.

The eventual success of the Special Markets project allowed Mack to grow Pepsi into a major American brand by the time he left the company in 1950. What's more, his inspiration—his vision for the company—resulted in thousands of new hires for the company, people who would grow to *own* their jobs.

It's pretty easy to conclude that Pepsi's tremendous growth during Mack's stewardship wouldn't have happened without his employment of the Special Markets department. And the Special Markets department wouldn't have been so successful if each and every one of them hadn't fully understood and embraced the company's *Goal*.

What was the *Goal*, you ask? Aggressively marketing Pepsi— without changing the cola's mission of being an All-American brand of refreshment—to a whole new demographic.

---

2   nextreads.com/display2.aspx?recid=3590324&FC=1

What demographic was it? The "Negro market."

Though African Americans represented millions of potential consumers and many more millions of dollars, major American consumer goods companies largely ignored them at that time. Therefore, Mack hired Mr. Herman T. Smith, an African American, and shared with Smith his vision for Pepsi in the coming years, what Pepsi stood for and represented, and how it fit in the American lifestyle. Then he gave Smith—as well as a couple of African American interns named Allen L. McKellar and Jeanette Maund—their mission: **sell this product called Pepsi to African Americans across the land.**

After that, it was up to the people Mack hired to figure out the best way to achieve the *Goals* that were set out before them.

The members of the Special Markets sales force would have to be imaginative. As African Americans, they had to overcome the difficulties of traveling across the nation and finding places to stay for an evening or somewhere to enjoy a meal. They had to sit in the back of buses. They had to occupy separate train compartments. (I would ask you to note that this project began years before Jackie Robinson broke the color line in baseball.) The Pepsi salespeople had to develop and place advertising that would depict African Americans drinking Pepsi and making it a part of their lifestyles...lifestyles that compared favorably with the wholesome vision of the brand laid out by Mack.

It was up to these traveling salesmen and women to overcome segregationist obstacles they encountered on a daily basis and attract an entirely new market to their product—which they did, earning millions of dollars for Pepsi and for themselves. In fact, in 1962, one of the department's salesmen, Harvey Russell, became the first African American to achieve the title of Vice President at a major American corporation.

Walter Mack inspired Smith and his staff of sales professionals to buy into his brand vision and gave them a clear job to do, a job that was theirs to own. They knew, without uncertainty, hesitation, or doubt, the *Goal* to be achieved: *Sell Pepsi to African Americans*.

Their success would be gauged by that metric alone. More importantly, they believed in the *Goal* and felt the result was theirs to achieve. They *owned* their jobs, and they owned the result of connecting Pepsi to that specific *Goal*.

Being in leadership, you know you have to set goals not just for yourself, but also for your company. That means you must also set goals for your employees. Mack didn't just happen upon his *Goal* for the Special Markets team; he didn't throw darts, and he didn't pick the team's goal out of a dozen potential goals he'd thrown into a hat. Mack did a lot of hard work, a number of hours of thinking, and months of planning before bringing his Special Markets team together.

He then shared that *Goal* with the people who would work toward it and execute it. Mack knew that the *Goal* he developed *would define the Special Markets team and its success or failure*. By making that *Goal* succinct and easy for people to understand, Mack was able to turn that one simple *Goal* into the single thing that his Special Markets worked to achieve.

Goals can be big things. *Goals* can be small things. *Goals* are whatever things you want your business to achieve. *Goals* have to be easy to impart to your employees. *Goals* must always, and in every way, align with the overall mission of your company or else the *Goals* will not be believable and will not be met by your employees.

Harvard Business Press published a blog entry by Cornell University's Distinguished Professor of Corporate and Business Law, Lynn Stout, entitled, *Why Do Corporations Need a Single Purpose?* In the article, Stout writes that companies need a single purpose not based on law, but as a measurement tool to decipher how the company is performing. Her dramatic point in the article states that if you don't have a common purpose, people will run "amok," following their own paths, perhaps thinking that what they're doing is right, or perhaps doing just about anything to keep from getting fired.

In her article, she quotes Harvard Business School's Michael Jensen:

> *Any organization must have a single-valued objective as a precursor to purposeful or rational behavior... It is logically impossible to maximize in more than one dimension at the same time...telling a manager to maximize current profits, market share, future growth profits, and anything else one pleases will leave that manager (employee) with no way to make a reasoned decision. In effect it leaves the manager with no objective.*

I grew up near Harvard, but that's about as close as I'd ever get to the revered school. I don't even own a tweed jacket with patches on the elbows. I am, however, smart enough to understand Stout's point. Alignment around a common, purposeful *Goal* dictates employee behavior, in essence, forcing them to make the right decisions for the organization, while allowing them to feel that they are part of the plan, part of the mission. It's a thing of beauty.

A mission is the overarching reason why a business organization exists. A *Goal* is anything that helps a company achieve that mission. Leaders who understand this line of thinking succeed. That's because a person who develops a *Goal*, and gets a staff to buy into that *Goal*, is the very definition of a leader—a person who others follow, because they believe in achieving the *Goal* as much as the leader does.

When a *Goal* is not defined by a leader, or bought into by her employees, an organization has no singular focus; and the right goals are not achieved.

The leader's job is to define what's important, not the other way around.

TRUTH GRENADE: *Goals* **unite. With a** *Goal*, **your team has a reason to come together. Without a** *Goal*, **they're just employees doing what they're told to do.**

10

DEFINING YOUR "X"

IT'S easy to sit back and say, "We need a *Goal*." But how do you define it in a way that's simple, believable, clear, and, most importantly, inspiring?

I call it defining your "X"...your objective, your *Goal*. You would be amazed that most organizations don't know what their X is. They have no idea what they're really in business to do, for whom they do it, or even why they do it. In addition, the company's leaders, who have been leading the company for decades, cannot agree on how they see the company or its goals. Not only that, they can rarely agree on exactly why the company does what it does, which makes it extremely difficult for them to adequately and systematically define a purpose so clear and so powerful that it will change employees' behaviors.

With a specific *Goal* in mind, we could (and would) change our behaviors even further, knowing that something is doable, measurable, and needed.

Goals give purpose, change behavior, and, most importantly, provide the needed direction to individuals and groups who need that clear direction.

When consulting with aimless companies who lack a clear, identifiable mission, I set out to help them answer "existential" questions before they ever consider "executional" or "operational" questions. Answers to the former provide the *Why*, a foundation upon which the company exists. Answers to the latter questions provide the *Goals*, the things that people can do to answer or fulfill the *Why* and fulfill the company's mission.

If I were to be retained by Southwest Airlines (full disclosure: I'm not, but I'd like to be), I imagine this first step in the consultation—this finding of the X—would be a perfunctory exercise. Southwest's mission is as clear as a Colorado day. Everyone there knows it. Everyone lives it. It forms behaviors, drives employees, and creates organizational policies to which everyone in the company adheres.

Southwest's X is "to be *the* low-cost airline." Period.

Very few businesses are as clear about their missions as Southwest Airlines is. That's why finding the X is often so difficult, so important, and so enlightening. When members of a leadership team have a difficult time determining their company's X, they seem to have a mirror turned on them for the very first time.

Only after some long-winded, meandering dissertation about the organization and how they value their customers and their employees, only after leaders explain that their company makes life better for everyone involved in it, and only after they stop shoveling pabulum about their company's altruistic values, can leaders really look in that mirror and see what's missing.

That's the REAL starting point! Finding the X is the point at which leadership is able to separate what is important from what isn't. It's also the point where many people in leadership realize that they've spent far too much time on activities that not only don't fulfill the mission of the company, but also don't promote any concrete goals. It's the point at which the business is laid bare. It's at that point that company leadership can begin to answer questions, such as, "What is this year's priority, and what do you need to do to hit it?" That's when the fun begins.

With very few exceptions, the people we speak to at some of the world's biggest companies respond to those questions with raised eyebrows, a shrugged shoulder, and a shaking head. The stuttering that accompanies just about everyone's answer starts with, "Ah...I guess it's...well...."

I always respond with a knowing grin. One cannot overstate the importance of a single-focused *Goal* that helps your company fulfill its mission.

Many companies have a mission statement. Far too many are wordy messes that appear to be written by a band of attorneys for a tobacco company. They're not Mission Statements. They're responsibility-dodging documents. A mission statement is simple, or at least should be. It states who you are and why you're here. Once again, think Southwest Airlines.

TRUTH GRENADE: Go read your company's mission statement. Wait five minutes. Chances are you can't recite it—not even one word.

If you haven't defined your mission, and thereby written your mission statement, start by answering these questions:

- Why are you in business? What is the core reason you're there? For whom do you do it?

- What do you stand for? What do you hold so important that, if you changed it, it would devastate your company?
- What do you do better than your competition? What do you need to do to be better than your competition?
- If you had to choose, what one thing must you accomplish to be successful?

Now, based on what you've said, do you have the right people to help you achieve your goals?

In something as diverse and dynamic as the business world, you have to define some very simple things for your company or your department: When do we know we've won? What does winning look like? What does it smell like?

Call it corny, if you want; but you seriously have to develop a plan for winning that you can clearly impart to each of your employees. Only then can each employee understand the context of his or her responsibilities. It's the first brick on the path you are building to develop *Job Owners*.

The company mission and the *Goals* that help people fulfill that mission need to be clear and concise. They need to be easily communicated to employees, clients, and potential clients. They need to be attainable. To that end, I make sure that my clients' employees are able to finish each one of these sentences:

- Our mission is to…
- Our competitive advantage is…
- Our advantage over our competitors is…
- The business processes critical to our success are…
- Our long-term strategic plan is to…
- Each department's role in achieving that strategic plan is…
- Our immediate goal in the next twelve months is…

Once again, a *Goal* can be anything. But it's up to those of you in leadership roles to make sure it's tangible, definable, important enough that people want to get behind it, and easy enough for everyone to get their heads around. And, finally, it needs to seamlessly fit within your company's mission.

To ensure you and your employees are able to achieve the *Goals* you have set out, you should:

- Identify any roadblocks that will impede the desired result
- Create a plan with *Goals* that, when met, ensures you and your team's success

- Involve individuals or departments by soliciting their input, then making your ideas better by incorporating their ideas
- Ensure that each person understands the mission, without any questions
- Ensure that each person understands, without question, *Why* the mission needs to be fulfilled
- Develop measurements that identify your success or failure
- Ensure the measurements are clear and that each and every person in the company understands and believes in them

11

CLARITY

WHAT are *Goals*? *Goals* are simply responsibilities that are put into action. Walter Mack turned over responsibilities to his Special Markets department, and those team members reached *Goals* he had set for them within Pepsi-Cola's mission and the vision he had for the company going forward. Mr. Mack's employees put responsibilities into action.

Even setting small, easily-attainable *Goals*—and meeting them—can lead to trajectory-changing business events, just as long as the message sent is the right one.

Consider the story of a department leader in a large marketing consultancy with whom we worked a few years ago. The owner of the agency hired us to observe, recommend, and generally ensure that what the management was projecting to its employees was the right message.

The leader called an off-site meeting of the eighty people he managed. He kicked off the meeting by saying that there are a few serious issues he had to discuss, some of which are getting to be a problem for the entire department.

Issue #1: Timesheets

That's right, timesheets. This leader is telling a group of adults—professionals between the ages of twenty-five and forty-five—that too many of them are consistently delinquent in turning in timesheets.

"Our time is what we sell," he belts out from the front of the room. "Our time is our product. Only by filling out our timesheets do we get paid by our clients. Get your timesheets in on time from now on—no excuses. That is the mission of this department from now on."

With that, he went on to give everyone in the room a stern look and then asked, "Any questions?"

To his amazement, the questions came...and came... and came. For a half-hour, this leader answered a series of mostly-inane questions involving different scenarios where employees could be excused for turning in their timesheets late.

A couple days later, the leader was asked during a golf game if many people on his staff were consistently late with their timesheets.

"About seventy-five percent. Some of them are three or four months late," he replied. "One guy left the company, and he was six months behind on his time sheets; we couldn't bill any clients for his time. Do you have any idea how much that cost the company? Too often I've felt like a babysitter rather than a department head, so right then and there I decided I was going to do something about it."

The problem with this department up to that point wasn't the leader, but the message that leader was delivering... and he only realized it after delivering the timesheet message. Turning in timesheets on time is a *Goal*...a simple and attainable *Goal*. His department's mission was much bigger, like delivering the best service possible to the client or always over-delivering on what was promised. Regardless, his message regarding this *Goal* was clear: "Get timesheets in on time."

Effectively getting that *Goal* across was a good start.

After I consulted with him about the importance of clear goals and the difference between his company's mission and the goals he laid out for people, he realized his earlier mistakes and thought about all the questions from the meeting he'd had with his staff.

TRUTH GRENADE: You have what's called the "Curse of Knowledge." Because you're in management, you have all the knowledge, and you think that everyone has the same information; but they don't! See to it that they do.

This department head went to work to make a list of all the subjects he'd covered during the off-site meeting. He jotted down as many of the questions as he could remember. He used them to define his real vision for the department in clear, inspiring, and achievable terms—terms that everyone would understand and would be able to buy into.

He then called another off-site meeting to discuss what he had left out—the *Why*—*Why* his department needs to become the most efficient, most client-focused one in the entire company. He used some research to relate why being efficient—like getting timesheets in on time and ALWAYS returning client calls on the same day—is important. *Why?* Because ninety-six percent of unhappy customers never complain...a majority of them simply take their business elsewhere.[3]

Armed with such facts, he could develop his message as to what the department's mission would be going forward and how each person in the department could meet Goals that would fulfill that mission.

Before long, the department was, indeed, the most productive and efficient in the company; and the only off-site meetings that happened subsequently were for the purpose of celebration.

This story is true. The initial off-site meeting had been the first time anyone in that room had heard the message from anyone in leadership about the fact that the company sells its employees' time and that clients pay for that time. That, in and of itself, isn't the mission of the company, as I mentioned. But it is the sort of information that needs to be a part of a company's definition of *Why* something as pedestrian as timesheets are so important to its business.

I have found very few companies who can define the *Why* or their *Goals* for their employees with any clarity—especially in a manner that employees both understand and believe in. The same holds true for you and your

---

3   returnonbehavior.com/2010/10/50-facts-about-customer-experience-for-2011/

company. Defining your *Why* means defining your true mission in simple terms, terms upon which each person in your organization can take action. Those instructions must be so crystal clear that, without exception, your people will know if and when the *Goal* has been accomplished.

Because filling out timesheets is such a menial part of anyone's job, getting employees to "buy into" it may be a tough thing to do. But it is a believable, attainable *Goal*. By couching the need for filling out timesheets into the overall mission of the company—"Our time is what we sell... our time is our product"—the leader was able to furnish his employees with a good reason to fill them out. And that was just a steppingstone to presenting them with other believable *Goals* that helped the department grow and fulfill its mission.

A great message is important; a clear message is better. But the delivery of your message is as important as the message itself. Only when you have determined your company's mission can you determine the *Goals* your organization must meet to ensure the success of that mission.

Remember the story of Walter Mack and the Pepsi-Cola Special Markets team and how he stated the mission for the upstart company, set *Goals*, and let his employees find the best methods for delivering on those *Goals*? Follow that example yourself and you will have *Owners*...not *Renters*!

12

WHOSE IDEA IS IT ANYWAY?

WE have a client based in Washington, D.C., who, for years, could not hit either its company financials or its company's sales plan for its well-marketed, highly-sought-after product. They asked us to help them achieve both *Goals* of sales and profitability.

After just a few hours interviewing employees and leadership, it was clear that no two people in the company were speaking the same language.

Leadership was defining the mission, in its terms, as clear, definable strategies they felt could be easily accomplished. The challenge was that—of the three departments responsible for the majority of the work behind achieving the mission—not one believed the *Goals* were either achievable or even important.

We introduced the group to a foundational blueprint that accomplished the *Goals* by building the structures piece-by-piece. We started with the end in mind and built what we define as "Pillars," the steps necessary to get from the starting point to the finished *Goals*.

In the case of this client, we knew the company wouldn't be successful if the solutions came from its management; they had to come from the rank-and-file. The *Goal* was the *Goal*—the company must grow twenty percent in operating profit, as lofty as it was.

We went to the team and asked them what they thought. The results were, and typically are, astounding. Not only did they have idea after idea, but they actually signed up for more than what the leadership team originally committed to the stockholders. The team came up with six Pillars that they knew had to be accomplished if they meant to hit the company's *Goal* of twenty percent growth in operating profit.

The six Pillars they decided on were:

1. They must have a successful launch of their newest customer-operating platform, which equated to 650 new clients.

2. They must improve their current clients' use of their signature software product by thirty percent.

3. They must expand into the "i-world" by developing three new, consumer-focused apps for mobile devices.

4. They need to create a Software as a Service (SaaS) division to support their new clients.

5. They need to improve internal training on their new products and improve the customer service for their field reps.

6. They must build an empowered team of people that believes in the company's mission.

These six objectives became their Pillars from which their goal of twenty percent growth in operating profit would be accomplished. Sure, there may have been other ways that they could have achieved their *Goal*; but the *Goal* seemed so daunting by itself. It needed to be divided into tasks that could be done with relative ease—small victories— that, in aggregate, could add up to the twenty percent growth goal.

By adhering to these Pillars, our client was able to realize its *Goal*. But that's not the point. The point is, it was the team that created these smaller *Goals*, these Pillars to success. That's the point!

TRUTH GRENADE: Asking your employees their opinions scares you. But you should do it anyway.

Several years ago, the buzzword—"buzz process" for many of our clients—was becoming a "Balanced Scorecard Organization." If you're not familiar with Balanced Scorecarding or a Balanced Scorecard company, you should be. It's a management process made famous by Robert S. Kaplan and David P. Norton in their article researched and written for the Harvard Business Review in 1992.

What makes a Balanced Scorecard so powerful? First, at its root, it is a performance management system that focuses the entire organization around achieving its strategy. Once that strategy is defined, the Balanced Scorecard process ensures ownership by every employee—CEO, leadership, management, and front-line employees. Employees not only know what to do, they know why they do it. A Balanced Scorecard is a top-down reflection of the company's mission and strategy; it is a forward-looking view of future success, as opposed to looking in the rear-view mirror.

Next, the Balanced Scorecard process integrates external and internal measures, not just a single view, such as profit or volume. It keeps the organization focused on the measures that are most critical to the success of the company's strategy.

Finally, Kaplan and Norton concluded that once the vision is clearly articulated, it should be *all* employees who define the strategies required to achieve the vision, focusing on four key areas: financial, customer-related, internal processes, and growth and development. They said—and I agree completely—that to link measurements to actions (strategies) for achieving the vision, the answers must come from the people who will be doing all the heavy lifting.

It's important to remember that the mission is only the beginning. Subsequent to that are the activities—the *Goals*—that you and your team must perform to fulfill this mission. We call them "business-forwarding" activities or Pillars that, if accomplished, ensure success.

How do you get to the point that the mission can be defined? It's a very easy exercise:

- First, a company must *identify* the mission.
- Leadership must identify what *winning* looks like.

- Leadership and employees must be *prepared* to deliver on that mission.
- Determine the *length* of time required to accomplish the mission.

Take a tip from Southwest Airlines. Make a commitment to send a perfectly clear message to each employee as to what your company is there to do and why it exists. Avoid using words like "and," "but," or "or." These are "weasel words," words that people use to avoid making the kind of bold statements you need to make as a leader if you expect your employees to meet their *Goals* and fulfill the company's mission.

Make sure each employee knows—without any questions—what the company's mission is. Then allow them to make the best determination as to how to accomplish their *Goals*.

ROLES

13

ROLES

NOT all jobs are glamorous; therefore, people who usually fill those jobs are people looking to move on to a better job or get themselves from point A (a stop-over job) to point B. But when a position is *owned*—be it a front-line position, cashier, barista, sales executive, or senior executive—it makes a difference for the whole company that everyone can see.

You would think that was the case when, twenty years ago, I ran into a Waffle House line cook who changed my life and caused me to write this book.

I was off to see my very first consulting client. It was only weeks after hanging out my shingle. I was running late, of course, and didn't have time for a bite of breakfast. In fact, I didn't even have time for coffee—making that morning the first without coffee since the pilgrims landed at Plymouth Rock.

I drove sixty miles to my 6:30 a.m. meeting. The meeting went well; and I decided to grab something to eat before heading to the Worldwide Headquarters of Dahlstrom Entities, Consulting Group. I noticed a Waffle House about twenty miles back toward the office; you know...the outfit with the iconic yellow W-A-F-F-L-E H-O-U-S-E sign on the side of freeways across the country.

Once there, I hesitated to get out of my car, as there was a line of people that literally went out the door. It wasn't a Sunday brunch crowd. This was a Tuesday, and it was about 9:30 in the morning. Yet people were clamoring to get in!

Luckily, I was able to grab one of the two empty seats at the counter, asked a waitress for the cup of coffee I'd been longing for all morning, and ordered waffles and sausage.

Now, you've probably seen a Waffle House, even if you haven't been inside one. For the most part, they're all pretty much the same, with an open kitchen in the middle, a lunch counter surrounding it, and booths sitting along the plate glass walls that separate the Waffle House from the parking lot.

Between the counter and the kitchen of this particular Waffle House was a walkway that was about eight feet wide, with a narrow (about two inches) yellow line surrounding the entire kitchen. Outside the yellow box stood a number of waitresses in a line.

The waitress who'd taken my order stood in line with her fellow waitresses to my left. She didn't say a thing; rather, she glanced at the people who were sitting at the counter to assess whether or not any of them needed her attention. Occasionally, she'd look just ahead into what could be called the kitchen, where one person—a kid who couldn't have been more than nineteen years old—was flipping flapjacks, cracking eggs, pulling biscuits out of the oven, and plating orders.

For the most part, the kid's head was down; and he was very intent on his job. Occasionally, he would step to his left or right to get something; but most of the time he was stationary, working in front of the intense heat of his industrial gas stovetop, while a fan over his head pulled up the smoke.

The kid quickly placed about a half-dozen completed plates upon the counter in front of him. Then the waitress at the front of the line gathered them up and delivered them to a booth table.

No sooner had the cook completed the order, than he made eye contact with the next waitress, who belted out with a staccato delivery, "One regular 'Papa Joe's Pork Chops and eggs,' one 'Toddle House Omelet,' a 'Fiesta,' and one 'Strawberry Waffle' with a side of large Country Ham." The cook nodded to the waitress as she took a step forward, inside the yellow line. The waitresses behind her moved up to wait for their orders.

Moments later, the cook presented that waitress with three plates full of food, plus a large side order of Country Ham.

The waitress quickly removed them and delivered the order to her customers. The line of waitresses moved again toward the middle of the counter, and the one in front waited until she got the kid's attention.

I continued to watch the cook—this single kid—listening to an order, committing it to memory, and delivering it to the waitress who'd placed the order in a matter of minutes... sometimes seconds. There were no questions. There were no squabbles. There was very little communication or interaction beyond the orders themselves. The kid was calm, and his actions were compact and purposeful. His aura was in total contrast to the bustling activity throughout the rest of the Waffle House.

Waitresses, when they weren't waiting calmly outside the yellow line before the cook, were moving quickly throughout the restaurant delivering food and refilling coffee cups.

When my order was delivered, I asked my waitress to give the cook a message.

"What's on your mind?" she asked quizzically.

"Tell him I want to buy him a cup of coffee when his shift's done."

The waitress said she would, but couldn't hide the touch of suspicion on her face. Then she warned, "It'll be about an hour...after the rush."

"No problem." I finished my meal, enjoyed another cup of coffee, and spent the next hour watching the well-choreographed Broadway production that was taking place in front of me. Everything happened for a reason. Every movement led to another. Everyone did his or her job flawlessly, and the kid in the kitchen orchestrated it all.

An hour later things had settled down. The kid came out from behind the 500-degree oven and said, "Jennie says you want to buy me a cuppa Joe."

I didn't even attempt to shake hands. It was obvious that he wasn't used to meeting customers; he didn't roam the dining room like some restaurateur. He was just a guy doing a job.

"Hi," I said, introducing myself. "I couldn't help but watch you back there. That was an awesome display. How do you do it?"

"Huh? What do you mean? You think that was something special?"

"Unbelievable," I said flatly. "You didn't write anything down, you didn't screw up any orders, and every customer got exactly what he wanted minutes after the order was put in. No customers left anything on their plates—do you know how rare that is?"

The kid pushed back from the counter, shook his head, and scratched his nose with a long, bony finger. He looked around as if expecting one of his co-workers to come rescue him from this situation. Realizing he was on his own, he shrugged his shoulders and let out a weak, "No."

"I've worked in restaurants my whole life," I said. "I know how hard it is to do what you do. How do you do it?"

The kid was looking really uncomfortable. "Welllllll...," he droned. "The girls tell me the order; I remember it; I get it out. It ain't rocket science. It's work. Simple." He looked a little annoyed, but stayed put.

"Simple?"

The kid suddenly took on an air of confidence. His expression changed, his chin shot out, and he seemed to burst with pride. Then he leaned on the counter, right in front of me, and said, "Man, I *own* this job."

"You *own* your job?" I repeated. I'd never heard of anyone saying he *owned* a job...a business, sure, but a job?

"I *own* my job. I *own* everything that happens within that yellow line," the kid motioned at the yellow line on the floor and pointed as if to punctuate his point. "I'm responsible for everything that happens inside that yellow line. I'm responsible for hot food, done correctly, without screwin' it up. Everything outside it is someone else's responsibility, and I don't worry about what happens outside the yellow line at all. That's the way my manager trained me, see? I take care of everything within that yellow line; everyone else can take care of their jobs outside that line, and the restaurant keeps doin' a great business."

The kid wasn't just a cook. He wasn't just an employee. He was an *Owner*. He *owned* what he did. He *owned* how he did it. He had the power within his boundaries of the restaurant— within the whole Waffle House corporate entity—to figure out the best way to deliver every order. He did the job he *owned*. Everyone else did the jobs they *owned*.

Every morning every single Waffle House in the country is packed with diners, and the company's investors receive value for the capital they've put to work in the Waffle House and its franchises. So why does this particular Waffle House work so well? It works so well, because each person who works there knows his or her responsibilities and his or her *Role*. The kid, for instance, knew that everything inside that yellow line was his responsibility. And everything that happened outside the yellow line...not of any concern to him.

TRUTH GRENADE: If you were asked to find the yellow lines for each of your key employees, chances are you couldn't—and neither could they.

The training and communication of responsibilities had to be clear to the cook (and the servers) from the minute he showed up for his first day on the job. The responsibilities and *Roles* of the job he was filling—all crystal clear. In return, the kid understood what was expected of him and went on to perform his responsibilities in the best way he could. He knew his *Role* and understood where it fit in the scheme of that particular Waffle House franchise and, likely, in the whole 1,700-restaurant Waffle House entity.

And what about the kid's boss? What about the manager of the Waffle House? He didn't have to help the kid with orders; he didn't have to help the wait staff with cleaning up tables and preparing them for the next guests. That's because the manager of this particular Waffle House had likely already done his job with this crew; he had articulated what was expected, each person's individual responsibilities, and everyone's *Role* within the overall vision and mission of the Waffle House. He hired the right people, got them to buy in, and let them *own* their jobs.

That's the way everyone who works for you should work.

The way I looked at it, the kid's boss had put into play all pieces that set him up for success:

- He had a defined *Role* and defined expectations; he knew exactly what was supposed to happen inside and outside the "yellow lines"
- The kid fully understood and bought into the company's objective

- His boss removed any obstacles that might get in the way of the kid being successful; waitresses did their jobs to ensure he was able to do his

- He got out of the way!

It's up to you to draw the yellow lines for your employees.

14

ACCOUNTABILITY: BUSINESS'S FOUR-LETTER WORD

ALL of this sounds great, doesn't it? Building a company full of *Owners* is as simple as defining the *Goal* and then defining the *Role* of the employee within the boundaries of the mission. Simple, right?

Not so much.

Not every employee will take the proverbial bull by the horns and suddenly become responsible. Some will rise and take an *ownership* position in their jobs. Others will take advantage of the situation and do very little on purpose, and still more employees might sit idly by looking for more direction. Hey, it's a pretty good bet that no boss has ever presented a new hire with his or her new job by saying, "You own your job." A new hire may be thinking, "How can I *own* my job? I just got hired, and my first day is still two weeks away."

The concept of *Job Ownership* brings with it another very important aspect: accountability. Your employees have to be accountable...but not to you. Expecting them to be accountable to you is an invitation to conflict. Sure, they need to be accountable to the standards that you expect them to uphold. But they have to be accountable to themselves by what *they* define as accountability.

The concept of accountability has been tossed about by leaders good and bad since Noah first saw a storm cloud and began gathering wood. Or did he, like so many people who take a leadership role, begin overseeing the building of his ark by others?

Too many leaders tell people to be accountable, but never explain what that means. Employees try to be accountable, but never know if they're covering all the bases.

The most important thing about accountability is that everyone agrees on exactly what accountability looks like. Who is accountable for what? Where are the boundaries? Where are the opportunities? Where does one person's accountabilities end and another person's begin? (This last one is very important! Don't overlook it. Remember the Waffle House story.)

The first step in accountability is recognizing responsibility. It could have been one of Noah's employees who was responsible for bringing as many pairs of animals to fit on an ark as possible. It could have been another employee who was responsible for gathering the wood to make the ark. Each individual on the team must understand his or her *Role* and make a conscious decision that it is ultimately up to him or her to do the job and become an *Owner*. Once again, this needs to happen within the context of the company or team's vision.

You might ask, *"How, though? How do I get people to actually be accountable?"*

Make no mistake: accountability starts and ends with you. It's *you* who needs to spell out who is accountable for what. You and your employees need to agree on accountabilities so that both of you know what needs to be done and by whom. You need to make sure that accountability is about something bigger than the employer/employee relationship. An employee won't be accountable solely because you have the power to let him or her go. You need to make sure that the people who report to you are perfectly clear about who's accountable for what.

Secondly, you and your employee should always write down all accountabilities together. You do this by first asking your employees to write down their own accountabilities; it's great preparation for a very interesting conversation. Because they finally have the opportunity to write a set of responsibilities and believe they do a whole bunch more for the company than anyone ever gives them credit for, chances are they will overcommit. Or it could be that their ideas of how they're accountable is so different than yours that you will be faced with a terrific conversation about exactly what you *expect*.

Expecting them to be accountable to standards that the *two of you agree* upon makes them accountable to something bigger than you, a superior; it makes them accountable to their own word and a level of performance to which they have agreed.

When an employee is accountable to a level of performance that he or she has helped define, that employee is proud to let you "inspect what you expect." If you try to inspect what you expect from an employee who hasn't bought into a *Role*, a project's *Goal*, or the company's mission, you'll get resistance. You'll also get something short of the results you want and probably something short of the results that the employee is capable of.

So what is the process of holding people accountable? Accountability is more of a result than an expectation when you, the leader, have done the groundwork necessary to fill your staff with *Job Owners*.

TRUTH GRENADE: Don't fool yourself; most people are never held accountable. Accountability scares the leadership of most companies.

No matter what kind of employees you have—adults who are long-time professionals or teenage kids just looking for Clearasil money—there is a checklist you can follow to make sure your employees are accountable to you and, more importantly, the job that they presently hold:

- Once again, ensure that every employee fully understands and has bought into the company's mission
- Allow the employee to define his or her own set of objectives to ensure the *Goal's* success and contribute toward the mission of the company
- Document

- Agree on deadlines ahead of time, and don't let them slip
- Create Key Performance Indicators that define your combined expectations
- Use agreed-upon Performance Standards that you and the employee have written together
- Show appreciation—employees need to know they're appreciated
- Inspire trust

15

EXPECTATION CONVERSATION

WHAT "Defining Roles" really means is "Defining Expectations." At the start of every project, we have the "Expectation Conversation" with all employees who are involved. We establish what is expected of each individual and make sure that each individual understands what is expected of him or her.

Sounds simple, doesn't it? Establish expectations, relay those expectations to team members, and then watch team members meet or exceed those expectations. But it's not. Anyone who's ever played the silly "Telephone Game" as a child knows how a simple message can get distorted—somehow lost in translation. Red becomes blue. Up becomes down. "Deliver this package to 4th and Main" becomes, "Flush your wife's diamond down the drain." I don't understand why this happens, but it does.

That's why the Expectation Conversation is so vitally important; it's the chance for a leader and an employee to speak the same language, as it were. It's when you, the leader, spell everything out.

Don't blow this opportunity! Make sure that your employees hear the same thing that you're saying, and don't end the meeting before you're confident that they do.

Results come from meeting *Goals*. People can only meet *Goals* that they know about and understand. So you, as a leader, must realize how important it is to define the *Goals*.

In brief, the Expectation Conversation starts off something like this:

"My expectations are for you to hit your monthly sales objectives a week ahead of schedule. My *Goal* is to show the division manager that we're number one in the region. I will give you guidance and help, if you need it; but I expect you to take complete *Ownership* of the process and responsibility for the results."

This conversation allows you to impress upon your employees that their jobs—the monthly sales results—are indeed theirs to *own*.

With clear expectations, your employees will have an unmistakable direction of priorities, waste less time, and ensure that a project is complete, secure in the knowledge that they are one hundred percent responsible for the outcome.

Without knowing expectations clearly, your employees will waste valuable resources thinking they understand your expectations when they don't. Employees cannot go forward with any questions in their minds that you could have answered for them.

After that, it's your job to ensure both your actions and your employees' actions reinforce your initial defined expectations. Telling an employee to take *Ownership* of his or her job rings hollow if you're hovering over that employee and micromanaging every detail of a job or a project. That's "Helicopter Management"; and it differs from "Seagull Management" only inasmuch as—in "Helicopter" mode—you don't shit all over the employee's work before he or she is done and then leave.

Here's a true story to illustrate:

Nathan, the project manager for a large software client of ours, walked into his boss's office and said, *"I got your voicemail...and your message."*

Nathan was in the midst of a very big project for an important client, and his boss was curious about how things were going. The boss had left a voicemail that conveyed confidence, but said he wanted to talk about some upcoming stages. The concern in his boss's voice was picked up by Nathan, who quickly approached his boss to discuss things.

Neither one of them wanted any misunderstanding about what the project should look like when it was done. The boss was right not to wait until then to express his interest in the project, which would be classic "rear-view" management. At that point, there might only be regret on both sides of the working relationship.

Nathan responded to his boss's voicemail right away, because he wanted to make sure there was a shared vision. After a quick discussion, Nathan got back to the project, incorporated some of his boss's thoughts and ideas, and, as a result, the project wound up going smoothly.

This open discussion of responsibilities and expectations really happened and was a byproduct of the company's culture where ensuring alignment around the company's mission is built on trust. The "message" behind the voicemail wasn't cryptic, and there was no need for a silly kabuki dance between the two about responsibilities regarding the project. That kind of thing only serves as a "CYA moment" for both people involved.

Everyone knows what CYA means. It's one of the great overused tools by leadership and employees alike in the business world. The CYA moment is a pre-emptive strike used by someone who wishes to maintain the ability to spread blame around if something under his or her purview doesn't work out as well as it should. It's the exact opposite of responsibility; and it's the perfect way to instantly lose any trust that's been built up, even if that trust has been built over many years. If you're a leader and you CYA at the expense of one of your employees, you have lost that employee's trust forever. In his or her eyes, you have shown your "true colors." Nothing you did before or will do afterward will ever overshadow it.

Nathan's boss could have let him finish the project and waited to see how it would work out. He could have "CY'd his own A" if Nathan's finished product wasn't up to snuff. But he didn't. The boss showed leadership by ensuring expectations were defined before the project started, thereby avoiding misconceptions, misunderstandings, or mistakes being made. Sure, he suggested some tactics that could be—and perhaps should be—used going forward;

and that was that. At the end of their conversation, they had a shared vision of what the project would look like.

Nathan had long before bought into the mission of the company and the *Goals* he had to meet to successfully complete the project. So stepping into his boss's office while a project was still in progress was no problem. He wasn't afraid of any threats—("If you don't get this right, you're in big trouble!")—because he knew that the company's culture included a boss who didn't wait for questions to become problems. Results were the focus.

There's an old saying about people who don't see the big picture...that they "can't see the forest for the trees." Leaders have to be able to see the forest; they can't get too close to the trees. Leaders need to have the proverbial 30,000-foot view of their business. Leaders have to know what success looks like a week from now, a month from now, a year from now. They need to know what results are required to ensure success, so they can communicate what "all the way to bright" looks like, as the old saying goes.

If you focus on the results of the mission, rather than every angle of how the mission is completed, then you and your employees will hit a stage of nirvana only Kurt Cobain could dream of.

It's the results, dummy.

Truth Grenade: Clear expectations don't simply define what you in leadership want done; they define priorities for your employees.

16

DEFINING MUTUAL EXPECTATIONS

YOU may recall the story about our client who called a meeting of everyone in his department and made filling out timesheets *Issue #1* of the meeting. Well, that's not all he did.

Sure, he opened a lot of eyes when he announced to his staff, "Our time is what we sell." But he then took full advantage of the fact that his changes had hammered home, for everyone in his department, a new perspective on their jobs—that they actually sell the *time* they spend working on a client's business.

He reviewed each job description that had been written for every employee in his department—job descriptions that he determined had been written during the '70s (perhaps the 1870s)—and re-wrote each one to reflect each employee's *Role* in achieving the department's mission.

We find countless clients with no job descriptions for any *Role* in their company. That's mind-blowing, I know.

TRUTH GRENADE: Stop reading this book now— right now—and ask yourself if you have job descriptions for every single person employed by the company. If the answer is yes, you are in the minority. If you answered no, you're the only one telling the truth.

The department head was honest enough to realize that he didn't really have any valid job descriptions for his employees. So he wrote them. Then he spoke to every one of his employees individually, taking each person through an updated job description and a clear vision of his or her *Role* within the department. He defined each employee's *Role* in such a way that it was consistent with the overall mission of the company. He also helped each employee understand his or her boundaries, as well as the opportunities that existed within them.

Such an exercise ensured that each of his employees shared his vision and was one hundred percent aware of how his or her *Role* would help fulfill the department's *Goal*...including the number one item at the top of every job description: Turn in timesheets at the end of each work week.

So what was his last task for achieving his *Goal* to align every employee around the department's vision? *Performance reviews.*

Few things in business are as universally unpopular as annual performance reviews. Grades are given and sometimes raises, as well. Areas of "opportunity" are recognized, and conversations take place that revolve around how the employee can be better equipped in the days ahead to be more valuable to the company. Reviews are difficult, time-sucking, uncomfortable experiences for everyone involved.

We've all had a few performance reviews in our day. Recall the story from the beginning of the book: *I was a terrible employee,* so you can imagine how those went for me. A day or two before the review, I would scramble around my office looking for evidence of work that I'd performed over the past year, whether it was client reviews or presentations I'd delivered. Once I located something that would help my effort, I would set the proof aside so I could use it like a prop.

Of course, all of my performance reviews went in a very similar manner..."*Matt, we're happy with your efforts here,* but..." (Here it comes) *"...we would like you to be less aggressive, etc...."* You get the picture.

In early 2010, the *Wall Street Journal* wrote an obituary for the performance review titled, *"Yes, Everyone Really Does Hate Performance Reviews."* The prestigious paper went on to say that performance reviews are really just a "...corporate sham, one of the most insidious, most damaging and yet most ubiquitous of all corporate activities."

Well, of course, everyone hates the review process. It sucks! The thought of sitting with your manager, who probably barely knows you exist, to discuss your past twelve months of company worth is bogus.

Unless...

Unless the performance review isn't a performance review of the employee, but is a performance review of the company and how the company is meeting the needs of the employee. Performance reviews are not just a one-way street. Performance reviews present an opportunity for everyone to be an *Owner*. You have to be held accountable for the opinions that your most important assets have of you. A review of anyone's past performance is so ridiculously important to everything you want to accomplish in your company or department.

So if you want *Owners* working for you, you should rethink your strategy. Let's face it: you give your employees feedback in an effort to help them get better at their jobs. You expect your employees to respond to your feedback— whether positive or negative—by becoming better employees for your company.

But couldn't you benefit from the same?

Employees who are *Owners* should have no trouble giving you feedback. Why not? They know the company's mission cold and can make suggestions to help you better fulfill your job within that mission.

Asking for feedback is the perfect way to learn if you've been successful hiring and developing *Owners* for your company. *Owners* know that they work not for you, but for a mission that has been spelled out by you and others in leadership. For that reason, any level of intimidation that "the boss" might have should be largely quelled; and *Owners* can engage in a conversation about different ways that the mission can better be fulfilled.

Sometimes the conversation can work as a mirror for the *Owner*, and sometimes it can work as a mirror for you in leadership. But perhaps the best aspect of management asking for feedback is the opportunity for *Owners* to manage up.

A leader who gets feedback from *Owners* is a leader who's not afraid to make adjustments in his or her management style. You also keep the all-important lines of communication open between leadership and the lower strata of workers.

Truth Grenade: You have never asked your employees how you're doing or even how the company is doing—and you probably won't start to do so even after reading this.

When I was laboring away at my first job out of college, before the one I triumphantly quit, I was working about twelve hours a day and not doing a whole lot else. The fact was, I wasn't earning that much money and was really more interested in working hard, getting better at my job, and earning more money in the future.

The president of my company had a tremendous policy where he took a few employees out to a bar for a "Total Quality Meeting" every Friday when he was in town. He'd swing by offices during the week and ask three or four employees to join him at a nearby bar at about 4:00 on

Friday afternoon to have a relaxed, hour-long discussion about work.

The company president was thirty years older, a foot taller, and many layers ahead of me; so when he came into my tiny cubicle and asked if I'd like to join him the following day, I spent the next twenty-four hours getting more and more nervous about sitting at the bar with the president and talking shop. What would we talk about? Who else from the office would be there? Would that cutie with the great smile from Marketing join us? How nervous would I be then?

Well, the cutie from Marketing did join us, as well as three other people who I had never met. We all sat at a high-top table; and after about ten minutes of small talk, the president asked me what I did that day to help fulfill the company's mission. I was a little surprised and very nervous; I'd done my usual "grunt" work and was planning to head back to the office, after our Total Quality Meeting ended, to do a couple hours more. I hemmed and hawed a bit before describing what I did all day.

With a little prompting from the president, I started to see what he was getting at. He kept pointing out how what I did helped other people and other departments get their jobs done. Suddenly, I started to have a better understanding of my place within the organization.

After the president engaged others at the table for a bit—asking different questions than he asked me, but still focusing on their place within the mission of the company—he begin talking about some of the initiatives he was undertaking. Even with the caveat that not everything he was doing could be discussed without approval of the Board, he did go through some of the projects that were presently on his plate.

Then he did a couple of amazing things. First, he discussed how what he was doing fit in with the things that all of us were working on. Second, he swung the conversation around to himself as a leader. He asked us what more he could do to fulfill the company's mission. A couple of people at the table had been to Total Quality Meetings before and were prepared for that question. I was completely taken aback. The president of the company was asking the people who worked for him how he could do his job better!

I joined this part of the conversation after a few others had gotten it going. By then I had lost all sense of being intimidated.

What ensued was about twenty minutes of discussion regarding the company, our clients, our vendors, and how our business could work better, more smoothly, and more profitably. Some of the comments caused the president to jot himself notes on a cocktail napkin (of course), where the best ideas are born. But for the most part, it was an opportunity for all of us to see how the company worked and where our positions fit within the company. The president of the company had put a mirror on all of us.

The following Monday, I had a note waiting for me on my desk. It was from the president of the company thanking me for the Happy Hour conversation and mentioning that he'd thought about it quite a bit over the weekend. I remember how that Total Quality Meeting made me feel better about the company all weekend long. The note made me feel even better.

The president of the company never lost touch with his 200+ employees; and his small actions made employees feel wanted, appreciated, and willing to do more. Furthermore, the president showed in his actions that he was always looking for feedback about how the company could be better and how its mission could better be achieved. He wasn't afraid to ask for feedback from people well below him on the company org chart; and he confidently proclaimed that when a businessperson stops learning about himself and his company, the business stops moving forward.

It takes quite a bit of confidence for someone in leadership to ask for feedback from the people who report to him or her. But I've found that it's vital to the cause of getting perspectives that no manager, no Board of Directors, and no president could get alone.

What he really did for me, without coming right out and saying it, was show he trusted me. He trusted in me, in my opinions, and proved my opinions mattered.

Call them Performance Reviews, call them Individual Development Conversations, or call them Total Quality Reviews. Call them anything you like, just as long as you call in every employee who works for you to have a two-way conversation about how it's going, whether the company is meeting the employee's needs, and if employees are still aligned with what the company is planning on accomplishing. Now is the time to ensure they know what you want to do, what your *Goals* are, and their *Roles* in accomplishing those objectives.

Oh, yeah, and I married that cutie from the Marketing Department.

17

LIGHT BULB MOMENTS

THERE'S a belief in the scientific community that most people use only ten percent of their brains. I have an addendum to that belief: "I believe the people who use just ten percent of their brains...are all those people in management." Seriously, I deal with people who lead companies all the time—I'm hired by them—and I'm constantly amazed by how many of these managers miss the most obvious ways to make their companies more profitable, more stable, and more successful.

One of the tactics I recommend is consistent and continued training of their employees. Don't just train them when you hire them. Don't just train them when you see a problem. Train them constantly. Train them consistently. What training really does is provide employees with information and techniques that they will find helpful in taking better control of their jobs. If you want a company full of *Job Owners*...you need to *train* a company full of *Job Owners*.

You don't hire a company full of *Job Owners*, you don't inherit a company full of *Job Owners*, and you don't wave a wand and surround yourself with *Job Owners*. You build, mold, and train an organization full of individuals who know nothing but what the company wants to accomplish and how what they do will help the company get there.

The world is always changing, and training helps do two very important things. First, it brings fresh perspectives to employees that they can't really get while they're doing their jobs and living their lives. Second, it clarifies exactly what is expected of them day-to-day, week-to-week and year-to-year. It *is* the definition of their *Role* while on the job.

"But what if I train my employees and they leave?" is a question I have heard. Of course, the best response (and one I've not had to say too often) is: "What if you don't train your employees and they stay?" I think the first fate is preferable to the second.

"Training is about transferring knowledge," insists Andie Hallihan of Applied Angle, a training and consultancy company. She couldn't be more right. Training is about providing employees with tools that they can use to make themselves and their companies more productive.

In 2004, the British government issued a document called the Leitch Report.[4] The gist of the report was that people stop learning at far too young an age. The Report lamented that this retarding of the learning process costs companies and entire economies millions of dollars—or pounds—in value.

Training is a way for management to bring in teachings, recommendations, and *Role Definitions* that employees wouldn't otherwise get. A trainer is a surrogate to management who presents and interacts with employees on management's behalf, but who also provides a voice and point-of-view that management can't.

What should you train your people on? Everything. Sandwich makers need sandwich training. Management needs management training, leaders need leadership training, and everyone needs training on exactly how they should be performing their *Roles* inside your company or department.

Truth Grenade: You might think you provide your employees with enough training—but you don't.

---

4   manufacturingdigital.com/people_skills/how-can-management-training-benefit-your-organisation

Are you training?

I have no idea what the standard symbol was for a good idea before Thomas Edison successfully presented the world with his light bulb...perhaps a torch. Who knows? Regardless, when we train trainers, I bring light bulbs with me and present them to people who figure things out for themselves. I call them *light bulb moments*—when you just simply get it. Every time I am (or one of our trainers is) working with a group, I insist that light bulbs must turn on throughout the day.

Here are a few things that happen in a Light Bulb Moment:

- An employee immediately recognizes what works. In doing so, he or she also realizes what doesn't work... kind of like Edison when he was inventing the light bulb.
- What doesn't work is not tossed aside. Some of what doesn't work now may work later. Having had the experience of figuring out what works to solve one problem can help the nimble thinker realize that the trail that took him or her to what works may need to be re-visited in order to solve another problem.
- The question, "What would you do differently?" always comes up. Why? Because people often feel stupid for having done some things that don't work

before getting to the place where they solve the problem. They shouldn't feel that way; but they often do, because they've figured out the best way to solve a problem. However, discussing what they would do differently usually sparks many more Light Bulb Moments for them.

People are naturally learning machines. That's why I get so frustrated when I see companies where leaders micromanage their employees, trying to make them little more than "wrists" doing the work that the managers dictate.

No one learns from that, no one gets better, and no one ever experiences a Light Bulb Moment.

18

STRENGTHS

IN his great book *StrengthsFinder 2.0*, Tom Rath writes, "We have a global obsession with identifying and fixing people's weaknesses. Management believes the best way to develop a person is by helping to fix what is broken."

Why not find employees' strengths and play them up? Kareem Abdul Jabbar wasn't a Basketball Hall-of-Famer because he could dribble the ball up the court, then make incredible no-look passes behind his back and through his legs to open teammates! He was a Hall-of-Famer because he and his coaches took advantage of his height and together worked on his skills as a center.

The first problem in just about every company is how the company is run. Does this sound like your company? You do an annual review with each of your employees, you identify what your employees are doing wrong—often calling these problems "opportunities"—and you create a plan to help fix them. Why? Would you tell Kareem Abdul-Jabbar he didn't dribble and make no-look passes well enough, then send him to the court to work on those skills?

I've learned from my experience with a large number of leaders, that that is exactly what you would do.

Why? Why turn the Kareem Abdul Jabbar in his prime into something he could never be? Use your employees' strengths. Take advantage of them. Those strengths became strengths because they are interests of your employees, as well as natural talents. Exploit what interests and talents your employees have, and you'll be exploiting your employees' strengths.

Strengths are not always easy things to find, mainly because people are rarely allowed to put them on display. In school, students are always told what they do poorly and what they need "to work on." Employees' strengths are all too often excused, as their managers push them to get better at things they don't do very well in the first place.

The second problem that I find leaders often have is a blind determination about an employee. Oftentimes, managers hear things through the walls and around the water cooler about a certain employee and adopt that stance. They don't make their own determination about the employee;

they simply take what was said about the employee and consider it fact.

Third, and most important, is that it's demotivating to the employee to constantly be told what he or she doesn't do right. That's a problem with so many leaders these days.

We all have shortcomings. Well, everyone except Tim Tebow, of course. But the rest of us all have shortcomings; and, in many cases, that's because we're asked to take care of tasks that do not play into our interests. Things we don't do well now will probably be things we don't do well a year from now. That's the way it is for you, and that's the way it is for your employees. Why bang your head against the wall? Why make work any more frustrating for your employees and for you? Play up your employees' strengths, and they'll more likely become *Job Owners*. Play up their shortcomings, and they'll likely become former employees, either by their choice or yours.

Whenever I come across a manager who dwells too much on his or her employees' weaknesses, I think about two guys I knew in college. Actually, one guy was me. The other guy was my roommate in my freshman year.

What happened with me—the experience that initially showed me the importance of playing to one's strengths—

was that my freshman year grades weren't very good. I wasn't sure why and remember wondering if college was really for me.

But I went back to campus; and starting my sophomore year, I started getting extremely high marks in every class. I was happy, I was doing well, and I was enjoying going to class. I realized I didn't need to stay up all night plying myself with coffee the evening before an exam, because I was already comfortable with the knowledge I had. I "aced" one test after another and even earned my way on to the Dean's List during a couple semesters.

Why did I "suddenly" become a better student? Was it something in the food they were serving in the cafeteria? Was it because I joined one of those advanced-placement study groups known as a fraternity? No! It was because I was taking classes that interested me. Freshman year found me taking a bunch of classes that were "required," while I was able to enroll primarily in electives during the rest of my college years—courses that interested me and that went toward my major.

Since graduation, I have stayed in contact with my roommate from my freshman year; and I remember when he got his first job out of college working in a company's sales department. Sales wasn't really a passion of his; but he got the job, and he was happy to be on a career track, while many of the rest of his college friends were still trying to get on the first rung of the corporate ladder. As the years went on, this guy did his job passably; but he wasn't setting any sales records, because, frankly, selling wasn't his passion.

When his company's website went down and word got to him, he asked if there was anything he could do to help. Unbeknownst to many in his company, he was an Internet whiz who spent many of his off-hours toying with video games and websites and also developing sites himself for friends' small businesses. This guy's expertise paid off quickly when he fixed his company's site and then upgraded it so that it would become a better tool for everyone on the sales force.

Where is my old roommate now? He's running the company's IT Department, of course.

Find what your people are passionate about, and turn those passions into advantages for you and your company.

19

PROMOTE THE BEHAVIOR YOU WANT

IT'S long been said that success has many fathers. It does not have many hangers-on, not many parasites, and not many passengers. Success has many fathers. Success results from many people taking the initiative and pushing the proverbial peanut forward.

To encourage that sort of *Ownership* behavior, the leaders of any company have to put it on display and show what the father of *Ownership* really looks like.

To many, that's you—the leader—whether you're a manager, a leader, or a business owner. To others, it's the individuals, your employees, or their peers. There is no better way to promote the behavior you want than by displaying it right in front of the masses. By showering with recognition those people in your organization who are living proof of what

Owners ought to be, you are teaching and encouraging others to do the same.

"Hey, I can do that. That's not that hard," should be said in the heads of every employee when you recognize his or her peers for *Ownership thinking* and *Ownership behavior.*

Truth Grenade: If we asked you to identify two employees whose behavior represents exactly what you want the entire organization to be— you probably couldn't do it.

Once the culture—that is the *Goals* and *Roles* of your company or department—has been established, it's up to leadership to bring everything to life. You, too, need to live the *Ownership* lifestyle. If you get to work on time, so will your staff. If you start your meetings on time, members of your staff will be there on time. If you finish what you say you're going to finish, the people who work under you will finish what they say they're going to do.

It really doesn't matter what style of leadership you practice, *the way you behave* around your place of business shows the people on your staff how they should act. How you behave is as much a part of helping your employees own their jobs as anything else, because behavior encompasses more than words; behavior is the way you bring your company's vision to life.

"Behavior is a key enabler,"[5] reports Dave O'Reilly, Chairman and CEO of Chevron, regarding how he gets the most out of his employees.

After helping your employees create the culture you wish the company to have, after getting them to buy into the mission of the organization, and after putting into place the processes to make that strategy work, it's up to you to present the behavior you expect in the workplace. Words are just words, strategies are just strategies, and processes are just processes if you don't exhibit the behavior that brings them to life.

Demonstrating the behavior you expect shows how the many people and the many cultures within your company can be integrated into an organization where everyone is working toward the same end. Promoting the behavior you want in the workplace can result in employees who really do have an emotional engagement with their work and their company, reports Brady Wilson in his book *Love*

5   unlockbehavior.com/

at Work. "Leaders who trigger emotional engagement release 400 percent more discretionary effort than those who trigger rational engagement."[6]

People react to the way they're treated. If they're treated with respect, they'll recognize the respect you're paying to them and reciprocate. One way you can show that respect, as well as gain theirs, is to hold yourself up to the high standards you expect from your employees. By showing them that you *own* your job, you'll also help them understand that they can *own* theirs.

The way you carry yourself at work is a direct reflection of the culture that you have helped to establish and will dictate the behavior you're trying to achieve. Making it possible for your employees to talk to you about expectations in their jobs, rather than begging for mercy, covering their tracks, and looking for excuses, is the best way for you to avoid having to clean up after something an employee does. Instead, you can engage in business-forwarding activities... like learning how an employee intends to tackle a challenge that lies ahead and providing guidance if needed.

Not only do Rear-View, Seagull, Helicopter, and other micromanagement styles slow your business's progress,

---

6 www.prweb.com/releases/2010/05/prweb3970234.htm

they also sap the kind of confidence you need to instill in your employees if they're going to *own* their jobs. You become known as a speed bump on the road to progress, instead of an enabler. If you develop that reputation, employees will avoid you whenever possible, depriving themselves of your expertise and depriving your company of the best possible outcome for a project.

Of course, a certain measure of rear-view management is natural. In your work, and in your personal life, you have probably thought about something you could have done differently or thought about what you should have said hours after a certain conversation. But if you want a staff full of people who *own* their jobs, you'll have to learn to overcome that natural bias.

You'll have to let go, and train your employees to operate under the assumption that you're not always looking over their shoulders. You'll also have to prove to them they work for a company where their responsibilities are indeed *their* responsibilities. Set up a culture where your employees know this, and you're well on your way to having a staff full of *Job Owners* who are accountable to the mission that you have laid out for your company.

Leave micromanagement for your competitors. Only a manager who has not taken the time to train employees, who has not gotten them to buy into the company's culture, or a manager whose ego demands he display his power over people, employs this technique.

Consistent clarity of message will be needed if you want a team full of *Job Owners*. It will be needed every day. Consistent clarity must not be misunderstood for repetition. Think about consistent clarity the way you might think about a television advertising campaign for an everyday consumer product like the American Express card.

For decades now, American Express has been telling Americans, "Don't leave home without it." Those of us who are old enough recall Karl Malden peeking out from behind his nose and imploring television viewers, "Don't leave home without it." That was a campaign that made him one of the top celebrity spokesmen of all time.

Since Karl Malden's days with American Express, dozens of others have made a pitch for the American Express card and reminded us: "Don't leave home without it." But why not? It's just a credit card. True. But, as their advertising has consistently shown every day, every month, and every year, Americans' lives are enhanced when they travel—or even when they're just running to the corner store—with the American Express card.

"Don't leave home without it." It's a consistently clear message that you've been hearing for years. It's also a consistently clear message that's been building a brand, building a business, and building partnerships now for generations. "Don't leave home without it." It's a tagline that's provided consistent clarity for years.

Consistent clarity is not repetition—it's consistent clarity. It works for America's great businesses. It can work for you.

ROPE

20

ROPE

WHAT is *Rope*? Why give *Rope* to your employees? What will giving *Rope* to your employees do to help them become *Job Owners*?

Rope is the room, the leeway, and the space that an employee needs to be given by an employer. With *Rope*, an employee can do one of two things. She can:

- Hang herself
- Figure out a better way to do her job, by making it *her* job

An employee who knows and buys into the company's mission and who also understands the *Goals*, and her *Role* in fulfilling those *Goals*, will use the *Rope* an employer gives her to figure out a better way to get her job done long before she fashions a noose for herself.

Never forget that your company is not a "jobs program." The focus of your company is not to provide jobs; your company's mission is to provide a good or service that you sell to your customers. Jobs are a byproduct. Jobs open up because you, in leadership, don't have enough time or knowledge to get everything done that allows your company to produce the good or product you sell.

Once you've done your best to attract and hire the best employee, once that employee has been trained and understands the company mission, you've got to give that employee the *Rope* to do the job in the best way possible.

Won't mistakes be made? You'd better believe it. But you'd also better believe that plenty of learning will be done— learning what, exactly, is the best way to get the job done.

How many times have the people who work for you done something wrong that has cost you money? It's likely that none of us can count that high.

When Thomas Edison was inventing the light bulb, he tried hundreds of thousands of ways to make his vision become a reality. He was asked many times if the process was frustrating, and he responded that he never became frustrated; he was merely eliminating ways that the light bulb would not work. He worked tirelessly to see what would work, what didn't work, and what he could and would do better and different next time.

As a leader, you should know your employees *will make mistakes*. They will overlook something, say the wrong thing, or do something that wastes money, for sure. They'll have to learn by doing; however, as many mistakes as they may make, they too may find the next mobile technology, Internet, or light bulb. And that's why you need to give them *Rope*—enough *Rope* to either succeed or fail.

Rope is about finding a better way to get things done, but not about *you* finding a better way. It is up to your employees to be empowered to the point where they know it is up to *them* to find solutions, find answers, and find a way to get the results that are expected. It should be steeped in your company's culture where everyone in your company knows that their jobs are theirs to *own*, and it is their sole responsibility to make the most of it. Once again, the job of providing *Rope* is yours. And it's no easy task.

Truth Grenade: Most managers are afraid of giving any *Rope* to any employees. Why? Because *Rope* says they're not doing their jobs.

This is the difference between the "want-to-do" efforts and the results they produce versus the "need-to-do" efforts and those results. Aren't you looking for exponentially better efforts and results from your employees? Of course you are. Legendary companies are born because employees are encouraged to put more into their jobs.

Witness Apple's "Blue Sky" program, LinkedIn's "InCubator," and Google's "20% time" policy, each designed to allow company employees to focus their efforts and energies on new ideas born from their individual creativity. Think of it like a venture capitalist investing money in an entrepreneur's vision of a great product or a great idea.

Google, for example, encourages each employee to spend twenty percent of his or her time working on something that is his or her own initiative—a new kind of software, a new kind of messaging system—anything. The results have been fabulous, as innovations such as Google Plus have grown out of the policy.

Of course, Google may just be following the lead of another company that's been in the innovation business since long before the concept of a search engine crossed anyone's mind. Minnesota Mining and Manufacturing (3M) has long had a 15% time policy, where employees could work on their own products and innovations.

Let's face it: there are "need-to-do" aspects of everyone's job. But 3M's 15% time and Google's 20% time help ensure that everyone can invest part of their workweek in a project that is truly something that they want to do and something they feel is important. These are also projects the employees feel will help the company grow and prosper, thereby enhancing their *Roles* and giving them a reason to further pursue those *Roles* and make them better.

The results of these projects have been astonishing. Of course, making discoveries and finding new uses for everyday products can be fun and seen as innovative by themselves; so perhaps it's easier to tap into someone's one hundred and ten percent effort at these companies. But how do you tap into one hundred and ten percent from employees in less "glamorous" fields? Easily...leaders who give employees the necessary *Rope* are really just instilling trust and confidence.

Rope is necessary for all employees in order to get the discretionary effort required. It doesn't matter whether that *Rope* is given to them in a formal way (like at 3M or Google) or if it's simply understood that every employee has the necessary *Rope* to make decisions for figuring out the best way to get the job done.

In her book *Unlock Behavior, Unleash Profits*, Dr. Braksick convincingly explains that many people have "...capabilities that are 'hidden' on the job."[7] Why is that? Perhaps because "the job" has a "ceiling," a limit as to how much that particular job is designed to contribute to the company's *Goals*. Management all too often looks upon a job as being just that...a spot on the org chart, a position from which they can expect the "grunt" work to be done so that other, more highly compensated employees can do the big thinking.

Making sure that employees have *Rope* means you have employees whose jobs don't have a ceiling. It means you have employees who are looking for new and better ways to get the job done or serve your customer. And your job is to provide a safe environment where the people who work for you know that you trust them.

As a fellow *lifestyler* and part of the NR, Tim Ferriss said in his smash hit book *The Four Hour Workweek*, "It's amazing how someone's IQ seems to double as soon as you give them responsibility and indicate that you trust them."

And isn't that what you want?

---

7   Braksick, Leslie Wilk, Ph.D., "Unlock Behavior, Unleash Profits," page 18

21

TRUST

WE met Ryan when we did some work for an advertising agency years ago. Ryan's job was to design print advertisements for a client that happened to be a microbrewery. The prospect of working on a beer account was attractive to Ryan, because, as a young man, he believed beer was one of the four food groups.

Ryan got his job before microbrews became "cool" and microbrewery advertising won awards for its irreverence and humor. In fact, microbrewing was a relatively new industry, one that many felt would get crushed by the "big" brewers.

Not too long after gaining his new *Role* of copywriter, Ryan was feeling disillusioned. Writing ads about beer wasn't nearly as much fun as drinking beer, but what could he do about it?

Ryan knew enough to tell you the difference between ale and lager, so he could clearly talk his way through meetings with existing and potential clients. Even though his client was glad to have someone as knowledgeable as Ryan on the team, the client still knew more about the business of beer and brewing than anyone at the agency did.

Up to that point, Ryan didn't fully understand many aspects of microbrewing, like sourcing of ingredients, how easy it was for one batch of beer to taste different from another, or what made the beer he'd tasted years before during a visit to Belgium so good. All Ryan knew was that he liked beer...and that he wasn't really having a good time writing beer commercials and ads that featured tried-and-fried phrases like, "The taste that no other beer can match," or, "Twelve ounces of true refreshment." Those marketing lines had been written by his boss, as well as the guy who'd held the copywriting job before Ryan took it.

It was obvious to Ryan, from his client's frustration, that an entirely new direction needed to be taken; and if the microbrewery business was going to thrive, Ryan would have to take some initiative.

So he did; he took some real *Ownership* of his copywriting job. He thought back to the conversation he had with his boss and the confidence his boss displayed in Ryan since he started at the company.

You see, Ryan's boss believed in giving his employees the *Rope* to either succeed or fail by empowering his people to think and act like *Owners*. He did it in a way that made an employee feel like he or she was the most important person in the room. Regardless of the situation or project, Ryan's boss always asked what Ryan thought was the best solution.

We repeatedly witnessed this interaction first-hand. Sometimes in a meeting he would openly say, "Before we make any decisions about the direction of the ad, Ryan, what do you think? Is this the best solution for our client?" Sometimes he would say it on the phone when Ryan had a concern or challenge; "I'm not sure, Ryan, what do you think is the best move for the client?" Regardless of the situation, Ryan's boss displayed the confidence and trust in Ryan that spoke volumes—to him and us.

What Ryan's boss knew was that it was up to him to define his expectations of his employees, giving them the direction required to do their jobs independently. Then it was up to employees to use the skills for which they were hired to deliver the best possible advertising.

Ryan's boss made the company's mission perfectly clear: provide the best advertising solutions to our clients that will help them achieve their company objectives.

Then he made the *Goal* of Ryan's work as clear as it could possibly be: "Your job (i.e. *Role*) is to grow the brewer's business the best way you see fit. Your *Role* here is important to the client's business, no matter what you do; because their success is our success. You are responsible for doing what's expected of you—improving the client's business through the right messaging."

Notice how there is not an "and," "but," or "or" anywhere?

So Ryan took his boss's faith literally. He researched and read everything he could find about beer. He subscribed to magazines that people who brew their own beer at home use to keep themselves up-to-date on the latest news and techniques. Ryan took tours of his client's brewery, as well as other local microbreweries. He talked to the brewmasters at length about the things they did to make their beer unique. He even used some of his department's expense account to travel to breweries in St. Louis, Milwaukee, Chicago, Portland, and northern California, because he wanted to bring groundbreaking work to his client.

Ryan's boss noticed his behavior. His energy and motivation was inspiring. Ryan's boss knew what was happening and encouraged Ryan to pursue all the information he could in order to "up" the quality of the work for the microbrewery.

Over time, Ryan's job became more and more interesting; because he was learning things about beer—his client's beer, in particular—that no one else in the agency had ever tried to know. He was able to impart knowledge to his clients, his co-workers, and potential customers for his client's product in a way that no one had ever done before.

As Ryan gathered knowledge, he brought more to his job; he expanded his *Role*. He began to write ads for his beer client that were more insightful and more informative to potential consumers than his boss or clients had ever seen.

Ryan's client was very impressed with all the new aspects Ryan brought to the business. So much so, that he also began to turn to Ryan—a copywriter in his mid-20s and the youngest member of the agency's team—as the resident expert on his own product and its competitors. The client asked for Ryan's input when he was going through the process of putting out seasonal brews or introducing entirely new lines of product. These were initiatives that wouldn't have been possible if Ryan had not tossed the boilerplate beer advertising he'd been doing into the garbage when he first got the job and replaced it with work that was fresh, unique, and award winning.

Ryan wanted to do more, bring more to his client's business, and write better, more insightful advertising for everyone involved. The way Ryan pushed himself, and the results of that extra effort, were evident to us. Ryan's boss had clearly defined his expectations for him—the *What*—and how his efforts would get them closer to the *Why*.

Before long, Ryan was teaching his co-workers about beer in a class he developed on his own. He not only taught it at his agency, but also at his brewery client's office and at the brewery itself.

Spurred by a desire to do something more with his copywriting job and with the trust and belief from his boss, Ryan:

- Understood his *Role* and his boss's expectations of the copywriting job
- Made himself indispensable to the success of his agency and his client's business
- Became the expert on beer and on his client's niche in the beer business, allowing him to *own* the copy and

concept when it came to communicating the client's mission

- Played a major part in fulfilling the *Goals* the client had for his product

22

R.O.W.E.

TRUST is like confidence. Both are difficult to gain. Both are easy to lose. Actually, trust **is** confidence. It's the confidence that other people have in you and that you have in others. If you're successful in gaining the trust of your employees, you will cultivate a staff full of people all working toward the same goal. Employees who earn your trust are as good as gold.

If you're unsuccessful at gaining the trust of the people who work for you, you will spend far too much time engaging in "rear-view management." This is the act of a leader backtracking on a project and essentially re-performing the same work that someone performed poorly.

Leaders also have a tendency to engage in other business-retarding behaviors, such as "Helicopter Management," which is hovering over employees and judging them on every aspect of how they do their jobs.

Either kind of management is bad management and will lead you to filling the same positions again and again, because employees are not allowed to do their jobs and *own* their jobs.

Focusing on the end result is the key to building an organization of trusted employees who work toward the same thing. As legendary author Stephen Covey once said, leaders should "...begin with the end in mind."[8] What is "the end?" It's the results.

Having said that, I am a big believer in a "Results-Only Work Environment" or R.O.W.E. You don't have to think hard to know what one is—it's a workplace where results are more important than anything else.

"Isn't that just the standard kind of work environment?" you may ask.

"Absolutely not," I can tell you.

If results were the most important thing for my former employer, then the MENSA member who'd been my boss would've taken a look at the results I was getting before telling me, "DAHLSTROM! STOP WHAT YOU'RE DOING, YOU MAVERICK!" I wouldn't have been told to "Slow down," or "Just stick with the plan," whatever the plan

---

8 profitadvisors.com/beg_end.shtml

was. He would have congratulated me on the results I'd achieved so far and likely would have told me to keep up the good work.

When a group of congressmen (speaking of MENSA members) secured a meeting with Abraham Lincoln to tell the President about rumors that General Ulysses S. Grant was drinking, the President quickly consulted the results Grant was having. Then he told the congressmen: "Find out what he drinks, and have a case sent to each of my other commanders."

As history shows, U.S. Grant was indispensable to the Union winning the Civil War. He was—as has been said of George Washington, Abraham Lincoln, and very few others—an indispensable American. What would have happened if President Lincoln, like the congressmen, had believed his General's fondness for drink was getting in the way of achieving the ultimate goal of defeating the Confederate Army and saving the Union?

I'm not about to equate my efforts for my former employer with U.S. Grant's contribution to saving the Union, but I will acknowledge that the General had an advantage I didn't have: He had a boss who found results more important than <u>how</u> those results were achieved. As it pertains to the Civil War, Abraham Lincoln probably put on one of the great shows of results-based leadership of all time.

Netflix, a company that's changed an entire industry in its fifteen short years of existence, has a unique take on the Results-Only Work Environment. Netflix allows unlimited vacation time to all employees.[9] That's right...unlimited... as long as the employees take the initiative to make sure their work is done and/or can be done while they're away. Basically, the company insists on results and expects employees to show enough maturity and responsibility to meet those expectations.

Far too often, management sublimates results; they're at the bottom of a list that includes such things as, "Don't rock the boat," and, "Fit in."

That's not to say a leader has to put up with insubordination or backbiting by an employee who produces results. But, as a leader, you do have to understand that results can be achieved in any number of ways, ways that you may never even conceive of.

---

9 fastcompany.com/1844184/traditional-vacation-dead-long-live-vacation

TRUTH GRENADE: Leadership is too often afraid to give its employees the trust they require. Why? You tell me!

23

LETTING GO

I'M not talking about "letting people go." I'm talking about "letting go" of employees—employees who are competent, qualified, trained, and ambitious—and allowing them to pursue results using their own individual skills. It's not easy for a manager to do. In fact, it's one of the toughest things for a leader to do.

The leaders at Google have gotten results, of course, in their mission of organizing "the world's information...(making) it universally accessible and useful."[10] But how have they done it? Aside from having a business model and mission that is unlike any company before or since, Google encourages employees to get results that aren't found in any business plan. One of the products that has emerged is Gmail, launched on April 1, 2004[11], as well as Google News and Google Talk. [12]

10 www.google.com/about/company/
11 eweek.com/c/a/IT-Infrastructure/Top-20-Percent-Projects-at-Google/
12 techcrunch.com/2011/07/20/20-percent/

Dozens of other products have been born out of Google leaders providing employees with *Rope*; and Google continues to post results, while making an impression on the world that no one could have predicted.

Leadership trusts the Google engineers to use their time wisely, and the engineers trust leadership to promote what they develop during their 20% time. This trust leads to results, and the results lead to an unqualified business success.

Your employees spend hours upon hours thinking of ways to make the place where they spend half their waking hours better. Allowing your employees the opportunity or latitude (to use a common business word) to showcase their passion for their jobs shows that you trust their abilities. This in turn gets you just one step closer to building an organization of *Owners*.

Let go of your need to over manage every detail of your employees' work lives. Ask them what they think are the solutions to your company's most vexing challenges. Chances are you will be surprised, and chances are you'll find that people start acting like *Owners*.

"For me," says Tony Hsieh, founder of Zappos!, "my role is about unleashing what people already have inside them that is maybe suppressed in most work environments."[13] The amazing thing about Hsieh and his company is that it started out, to the outsider's eye, as nothing more than a site where people could order shoes. But, Hsieh said, "We didn't want to just sell shoes...I was passionate about customer service."[14]

Shoes are a parity item. Hsieh knows that. Lots of stores, catalogs, and web sites sell shoes. Customer service, however, is a differentiating feature. A company that offers exceptional customer service is a company that develops customers who not only come back again and again, but who also act as evangelists for the company. Companies that differentiate themselves don't just gain more and more customers; they gain more and more customers who willingly take on the job of advertising agency for that business in their circles.

Zappos! also proves that when a company puts things in the right order, results follow. Many employers believe that if they offer employees more money and more perks, the employees will work harder, more efficiently, and become *Job Owners*.

Tony Hsieh and Zappos! know better. The company has employees earning as little as eleven dollars per hour on

---

13 brainyquote.com/quotes/authors/t/tony_hsieh.html
14 Ibid.

the front lines and doesn't appear the least bit worried that these employees are going to unload on its Zappos! customers about how little they are paid! In fact, it's just the opposite. These employees consistently outperform their contemporaries at Zappos!. Why? Because these customer service employees have clear-cut responsibilities and the *latitude* they need to make the job of meeting those responsibilities their *own*.

They go through an intense training program and are even offered money to leave the training program before they graduate and start their jobs as customer service reps. An amazingly low number of trainees take the offer. That's because, during the training sessions, they see the difference between Zappos! and so many other companies.

They don't get big paychecks. They don't get important sounding titles. They don't get much more in the way of material goods. But they get something much more important to today's employee: they are expected to *own* their jobs.

A few years ago a woman named Zaz Lamarr purchased shoes from Zappos! for her mother, who was in failing health at the time. Unfortunately, Lamarr's mother passed away before the shoes arrived; and it would be months before Lamarr could get around to returning the shoes.

When she called Zappos! regarding a return of the unused shoes, the Zappos! rep told her not to worry—the U.P.S. man would be by the following day to pick up the shoes and return them to Zappos!

But that wasn't all! Lamarr would also receive a full credit for the shoes she had purchased months earlier—no questions asked.

But that <u>still</u> wasn't all! After the U.P.S. man picked up the shoes to return them to Zappos!, another delivery man showed up at Lamarr's door with a bouquet of flowers and a note from everyone at Zappos! expressing sincere regret at Lamarr's loss.[15]

Is there a company directive that instructs the Zappos! rep to do such a thing? No. There's simply a culture that dictates reps do what they need to do to provide customer service that is unequalled in the industry. The rep didn't need to be led to the conclusion that sending flowers would be not only a humane gesture, but also a savvy gesture on behalf of Zappos! The rep already knew these things, because the rep was a *Job Owner.*

If you, the leader, start with the understanding that you need to provide your employees the *Rope* to fail or succeed

---

15 consumerist.com/2007/10/zappos-sends-you-flowers.html

and that it's entirely within your employees' power to take control of what they're doing within the mission of your company, you will have a team of full of *Owners* willing to do what it takes to do more.

Then watch your company take off on the wings of a staff full of *Job Owners*!

Truth Grenade: You're probably still not convinced that *Rope* is the best solution. Why? It scares you; that's why.

24

MISTAKES

I cannot say it enough: employees <u>will</u> make mistakes.

Even the best, most competent, well-trained professionals will make mistakes. Some will make mistakes of omission and some of commission. But they will make mistakes.

It is important that the lesson an employee learns when he or she makes a mistake is a lesson that allows him or her to do the job better the next time. Too often employees make mistakes, and their only thought is that they screwed up. They're afraid they're going to feel the wrath of leadership:

"OH, MY GOD! How am I going to cover this mess up before someone finds out? I'm going to be cited by senior management in a company-wide email as the company screw-up and the reason why no one will get any bonuses or vacations this year! I made a mistake! Nooooooo!"

Think such worrying is over-the-top? Of course it is. But it is the sort of stuff that will go through the mind of a young employee who has not yet tested the *Rope* he or she might have.

I remember a summer job I had working as a prep cook in an upscale restaurant. I learned a lot about food and business during the summers I worked at that restaurant; but never more than the morning I woke up at around 3:00 a.m. worried about something...something I'd done, something I'd forgotten to do, something I'd done wrong. What was it? Something.... For ten minutes I couldn't put my finger on it until—AHA! I had doubled the recipe for the cheesecakes I'd made the day before, but I'd forgotten to double the vanilla (a key performance indicator of great cheesecake) that I'd put in them.

I started sweating and got out of bed. I paced in my bedroom, while the floor creaked, until my brother threw something against the wall that separated our rooms and told me to go back to bed. I sat down and nervously fidgeted in the dark for a few minutes before finally turning on my light and picking up a book. I tried to read for the next couple hours, but didn't retain a thing. I certainly couldn't get back to sleep.

Just as the sun was rising, I hopped onto my bike and pedaled my way to the restaurant in record time. What would be my fate? Had the head chef seen the abominations I had created? Was he going to write me up? Had he elevated the problem to the manager or the owner? Would there be a note in my locker? Would the words, "Please don't bother punching the clock today," be written on it?

I was extremely worried as I sat by the kitchen entrance waiting for the day chef to open up at 7:00. "Doesn't your shift start at nine?" he asked me. I said it did, but I had a lot to do and wanted to get an early start. I was so disheveled that I doubt he believed me.

Once inside, I went directly to my locker. No note! I grabbed a coat and apron, punched the clock, and went as casually as I could into the walk-in cooler where I'd put the cheesecakes the day before. The cheesecakes were gone! The sweating returned. I looked around to see where else they could be...another cooler, perhaps? How about the trash bin out back? I couldn't look. Cheesecake was probably taken off the menu the night before, which would never be a good thing, since the dessert was so popular.

Just as I was pulling the collar of my coat in the same nervous fashion that Rodney Dangerfield made famous, the manager strolled through the kitchen door.

"Oh, Matt, those cheesecakes you made yesterday"—I tried to cut him off with my apology and throw myself at his mercy, but my throat was too dry for me to speak—"were unreal. We sold every piece last night and had lots of compliments. Can you fill up the cooler with new ones by the time we open for lunch today?"

With that, he cheerily stepped into his office; and I took a deep breath. Then I started making more cheesecakes. I even wrote a suggestion that we halve the amount of vanilla on the recipe card!

Had those cheesecakes tasted horrible when I took them out of the oven the day before, I would have quickly figured out why and made more using the right amount of vanilla. But they hadn't tasted bad. They looked as great as all the other cheesecakes I'd made that summer. That's why, in retrospect, I was so surprised that not following the recipe had struck me so horribly, while I would otherwise be sound asleep.

The point is I had plenty of *Rope* at that job, so I could make decisions on my own about the food I prepared. I could even put together a lunch special or dinner special based on leftover ingredients we had in the coolers. The bosses, the chefs, and the full-time cooks (who weren't going to be running back to college at the end of the summer) never resented my stepping into their realms. I brought value to the kitchen and helped them out during the active summer season. The result was that I could use the *Rope* I had and make the kitchen work more smoothly than it would if I weren't around.

And what was my reward? Actually, there were many. Aside from the fact that I would learn a skill I use to this day, I also learned how to handle responsibility.

All these years later, I still think of the leadership at that restaurant as some of the best I've encountered. It was a high-pressure atmosphere during the lunch and dinner rush, and everyone was expected to take care of his or her own responsibilities. If I was working the line, I couldn't shout down to the head chef that he was going too fast for me or surprise him by saying that I hadn't prepped well enough. So one reward was an appreciation of my responsibilities within the overall mission of the kitchen and the vision that the management had for the restaurant.

Another reward was satisfaction in a job well done. I got to the point where I didn't need to be told what to do or how to do it, simply because I had accepted the restaurant's vision for the quality of its food and service. I strived to fulfill that vision with every vegetable I cut and every Chicken Piccata I gave to the wait staff to deliver. If I made a mistake—and I made plenty—I owned up to it and did what I had to do to make it right. No one...not the head chef, the manager, or the owner...had to scold me.

An employee who has the *Rope* needed to own the job will not worry about covering anything up; that employee will think only about how to rectify the situation and how to do a better job in the future.

Truth Grenade: Chances are you have crushed an employee in the past. Why? Because you didn't see how mistakes are actually lessons.

Part III:

LEADING OWNERS

25

FAKING IT

IN 1994, United Airlines introduced something resembling an employee stock ownership plan (ESOP). Companies will use ESOPs as an added benefit to employees, often allowing them to make regular purchases of the company's stock and become owners of the company. There are also employee stock purchase plans (ESPPs) that allow employees to buy the stock at a discount. So if a company's stock is currently selling at $50 per share, and the ESOP calls for employees to purchase the stock at a fifteen percent discount, an employee can buy the stock for $42.50.

Much of the time, the money that's used to make the stock purchase is pulled directly from the employee's paycheck, just like the money that goes toward a 401(k) or 403(b) contribution. So purchasing stock in the company for which an employee works can be a tremendously easy thing to do.

The real goal of an ESOP is to literally give employees an ownership stake in the company for which they work. The purpose is that employees will bring increased pride and desire to their jobs and remain more loyal to the company, as owners tend to be. For the most part, ESOPs provide positive results for companies...big and small, unionized and non-unionized.

Early on, United's ESOP plan worked extremely well. Net income ballooned, profits rose, the stock soared, and its growing value helped defray the pain of the lost wages for many employees.

It was also a good time to be a shareholder in the seventy-year-old company, as United's stock was outperforming Standard & Poor's by sixty-seven percent and increasing shareholder value by over $4 billion. Employee grievances fell seventy-four percent. Revenue per employee went up ten percent. Surveys showed employees liked working at United; and workers compensation claims fell sharply, as did missed workdays.[16]

Employees were organized into system-wide, "Best of Business" (BOB) teams to iron out thorny issues, such as free pass policies for travel, figuring out ways to improve operations, and cutting costs. All of which "...made people

16 nceo.org/observations-employee-ownership/c/united-airlines-esops-employee-ownership

a lot happier, and the company was more productive," according to Corey Rosen, Director of the National Center for Employee Ownership. "But they didn't take the next step to institutionalize the process."[17]

The year 2000 was the last year of the ESOP, however, and the start of a disastrous period for United. The BOB teams were long gone. Pilots were negotiating for a new wage deal and staged a work slowdown that, combined with bad summer weather, led to horrendous delays and furious customers. United was starting to lose money, but wound up largely agreeing to the pilots' demands. Later, management also gave in to machinists' demands for wage hikes.

Basically, the ESOP wasn't a new way of doing business for United. It was a fad. A fad comes and goes, usually leaving us all wondering why we participated in it in the first place. Bellbottoms, Pet Rocks, disco...these represented a perfect storm of fads—none of which we hope to repeat.

United's ESOP should not have been a fad. It should have been the start of a trend that helped bring a new sense of *Ownership* throughout the company. United's management had introduced these changes in a cynical

17 articles.chicagotribune.com/2000-08-09/business/0008090281_1_pilots-union-wage-cuts-employee-ownership

way: the changes had a built-in expiration date. After that, everything was scheduled to revert to the way United was run before the ESOP was introduced.

And what happened? What would you expect?

Morale throughout the company started crumbling, as employees who gave up higher wages a few years back in order to own stock now saw the value of their holdings shrink. Many of them sold their stock into a falling market. For the next two years, things just got worse, as economic conditions and the 9/11 terrorist attacks severely damaged the entire travel industry.

United filed for bankruptcy protection in 2002; and while many factors contributed to the filing, the failed ESOP, and all the collateral issues with it, played a significant part.

Why did United's ESOP fail? Was it management's fear of employee ownership? Was it the pilots' and mechanics' demands for higher wages?

While the ESOP itself did not cause United to fail, the way it was set up didn't do anything to help United the way so many ESOPs have helped other companies thrive. The United ESOP was poorly administered by every account— limiting participation to only some employees and limiting the time during which the ESOP would be available. These actions were a signal to all involved that the company was not, in fact, doing business in a new way. The ESOP didn't signal a change in United's culture, but rather a temporary shift in the company's thinking; indeed, a fad.

What United attempted to do was trick employees into believing they would become owners of a company with a celebrated past and a bright future, hoping it would create the culture they desired.

Let that be a lesson.

Corporate culture is always—and in every way—designed by you in leadership. A positive culture is your responsibility. A negative culture is your problem. The "bait-and-switch" that United's management engaged in during the ESOP fad resulted in a culture that was worse at the end of the episode than it was at the beginning.

TRUTH GRENADE: Your culture is probably one that was created by default, not by design.

Your influence over and actions toward your workforce is what most drives employee behavior. If you're a leader who micromanages every move your employees make, you will have employees who require constant direction. Your employees will have no confidence in themselves or their ability to act on their own. They will not even try to *own* their jobs. If you're a leader who is honest and trusting of your employees, your employees—armed with the proper information and understanding of their responsibilities—will make the right decisions and take the steps necessary to *own* their jobs.

Do that and you will have a team of empowered people, people who believe the mission is important, worthwhile, and worthy of the kind of one hundred and ten percent effort you need to make your business successful.

For employee-owned companies to succeed, they need to combine broad ownership with an "Ownership Culture" that gives employees the information they need in order to have—and see—more influence in day-to-day decisions. Many organizations are afraid to share corporate performance data, foolishly thinking that employees armed with this information will smuggle it off to a competitor or hide it away in a black suitcase for a future date when their jobs are being held over their heads; and they can use it for leverage.

That's a terrible way to run a business! Information is the most important thing that any business can have. With information, employees will make better decisions. With information, employees will know what fits within your company's *Goals* and what doesn't. With information, employees will know how to make decisions within the framework of your company's culture.

Driving culture is what a successful leader does. If you don't drive your internal culture, you will inherit a culture by default, like that at United Airlines. United's leaders assumed that, by misleading their employees into believing they were buying a piece of a billion dollar organization, they would also develop a culture of *Owners*. Their plan was fatally flawed from the outset, perhaps mostly in the way that employees were expected to give something up for the right to gain ownership.

The fact is, employees at companies that offer ESOPs are generally paid more than comparable employees in non-ESOP companies.[18] Furthermore, a study from 2000 by Rutgers University revealed that ESOP companies grow 2.3 to 2.4 percent faster after setting up their ESOPs than was forecasted.[19] Due to the substantial concessions made

18 nceo.org/observations-employee-ownership/c/united-airlines-esops-employee-ownership
19 esop.org/

in exchange for the ESOP, the bitterness never faded among United's employees.

Neither labor nor management was ever fully committed to creating an *Ownership Culture* in which employees could participate actively in day-to-day, work-level decisions. Both sides tried out this approach in the first year, with the remarkable results noted above. At the end of that successful, one-year "experiment" with an ESOP at United, however, everyone reverted to the old ways of doing things. United's key leadership did not like the idea of the ESOP or employee involvement. Labor leaders had, at best, mixed feelings.

An ESOP is not a bargaining chip. It's not a temporary or partial benefit. It's not a fad.

Ownership thinking is part of the way you and your company does business each and every day. When you offer an ESOP, you're showing your employees that you encourage their ownership in the company; and you are letting them know that their services are worth more than a paycheck.

But most important is the fact that offering an ESOP is part of the culture you put forth; it's something that helps you develop an *Ownership Culture* in the workplace...

becoming employee-owned. It's part of the commitment you make to your employees and that your employees make to you. ESOPs need to be offered to every employee, not just a favored few or a group from which you need to score concessions. The leadership of United Airlines used the ESOP as a short-term tool, a way to get out of a jam. As a result, they got themselves into an even bigger jam.

Like the person who spends hours perfecting his golf swing or soufflé, employees who work in a company with an *Ownership Culture* feel a sense of pride in their work and in their company. The golfer makes every swing count, the cook makes every pass at a recipe count, and the employee makes every workday count. You and your company can only realize an *Ownership Culture* when you fully commit to developing such a culture.

26

HAPPY EMPLOYEES

SOME organizations have already figured out that *Owners* always do more than *Renters*.

Take a look at Red Bull, the iconic energy drink company. Red Bull is not only based in southern California, it's the embodiment of southern California. We consulted with Red Bull for several years. As mentioned earlier, we learned to be on the lookout, as we walked through their open-air offices, for a skateboarder delivering mail. The mail kid's favorite part of the route was in the C-suite, where the company's executive offices are set up below the half-pipe. Do you think this mailroom worker is a happy employee? Do you think he does his job as well as he possibly can? Do you think he makes sure no one else comes along and does it better? The mail kid at Red Bull *owns* that job.

An organization like Red Bull knows that happy employees bring a great attitude and productivity to their jobs. Their business is not just about marketing an energy drink; it's about promoting a lifestyle. They do it in their offices and with the lifestyles of their employees. They live the lifestyle they promote.

Author, Harvard graduate, and funnyman Shawn Achor speaks and writes about how internal happiness drives greater success than negativity does. It's his belief, and mine, that if you and I are constantly striving for more, then we never reach a level of satisfaction.

Happiness is not satisfaction. Rather, happiness puts us in a position where we strive to become more satisfied. Conversely, negativity puts us in a position where we're simply trying to apply the brakes on our runway of unhappiness.

Many people believe that once an employee achieves that new job or income level, that employee will be happier. In fact, the exact opposite is true. If you're happy first, then success comes with greater speed.

That's why companies like Red Bull—as well as 3M, Google, Zappos!, and others—put their employees in situations where they can't really help but be happy.

27

RIGHT TURNS

I have a client named Tim who has a story about what he calls, "My first real boss at my first real job." Tim was then a route driver for a soft drink distributor. He was hired to make weekly deliveries to a number of retailers all over San Francisco from Monday through Thursday. Then he had to spend Friday refilling inventories that had been depleted.

As you are probably aware, driving any kind of vehicle in San Francisco is a challenge. The streets are narrow in many parts of the city. There are hills and pedestrians to deal with throughout the town; and getting around in a delivery truck the size of a small moving vehicle with a full payload of products made each workday...well, Tim was just glad it doesn't snow there.

What made each day even more difficult was that Tim's boss was using new software that put together a map detailing exactly how he was supposed to drive around the city. It calculated approximately how long it should take to get from one retailer to another and how long the day should be before Tim would return his delivery truck to the loading dock down near San Jose. Tim's day would start at about 6:30 a.m. so he could get to San Francisco before rush hour, and he would return to San Jose by 4:00 p.m. for the same reason.

A month or two after taking the job, Tim was doing well, if not excelling. He was "hitting his marks," getting to his retailers at the times that his boss had predicted and returning to the loading dock on time. His boss asked him one day how everything was going; and Tim said things were going well, but that they could go better.

"How?" asked his boss.

"Your map is put together based entirely on going from one customer to another, because they're close to each other."

"But that's the most sensible way to make deliveries," replied his boss, as he went on to defend his map. He also went on to say that by following a major road like Columbus Avenue or Geary Boulevard on a particular day, Tim would best be able to use his time and the company's resources—i.e. the truck and the fuel—to fulfill his *Goal* of making all the deliveries.

Then he challenged Tim: "If there's a better way, you tell me."

During his two months on the job, Tim had noticed that simply going from one customer to another, because they were physically close to each other, was a waste of time and fuel in San Francisco. He was spending half his delivery days in a left-hand turn lane waiting for intersections to clear. He'd used a stopwatch one day and learned that he had spent two-and-a-half hours waiting to make left-hand turns. Maybe in Tulsa or Boise a bunch of left-hand turns wouldn't add a ton of time to a delivery schedule, but San Francisco was quite another story. So it was fortuitous that Tim's boss told him that if Tim had a better plan, to put it into execution.

Tim did have a better plan. He put it into action by laying a map of San Francisco on the table in his distributorship's break room, marking every delivery he made during the week, and developing routes that would replace left-hand turns with right-hand turns as often as possible. Sure, it meant that he'd be visiting the same neighborhoods two or three times a week; but the fact that he was moving more quickly from one retailer to another, and not sitting in traffic, meant that he was making the most of his time and the company's resources.

A couple weeks later, Tim was returning to the loading dock by 1:00 in the afternoon, with a gas tank that was only halfway depleted. His boss asked him to put together the same sort of map for other route drivers, and soon the company was much more efficient.

Who would think something as simple as eliminating left-hand turns could improve service and the bottom line at the same time? In this case, it certainly wasn't the boss—the person ultimately responsible for the company achieving those *Goals*. Good thing he felt comfortable challenging Tim to come up with a better system.

When you ask someone his or her opinion, the great idea that that person comes up with becomes the entire company's idea. Sure, it's still the employee's idea; and there's added burden on the employee to properly execute the idea. After all, it's an idea that employee *owns*. But when it's applied to what the company does, the whole company benefits. Asking for input says to your employee, "I trust you. I believe in you. Your opinion matters."

Truth Grenade: Just because someone—or in this case some software—says it so, doesn't mean it should be. Use your judgment about when to instill trust. It will pay off in the end.

28

THE FOUR MOST POWERFUL WORDS IN MANAGEMENT

IN the enduringly popular 1980s movie *Risky Business*, a high-school kid played by Tom Cruise is challenged by a friend to change the way he thinks. The phrase, "What the _____?" insisted his friend, would open up all sorts of new doors for him and overcome his inhibitions and hang-ups about his future.

"If you can't say it, you can't do it," cautions Cruise's friend.

Of course, what ensues is nothing any parent wants his teenage kid to engage in, like being chased around the streets of Chicago by "Guido, The Killer Pimp." But in the end, everyone and everything survives the adventure; and Tom Cruise winds up being more mature for the experience.

So how does a thirty-year-old movie about a teenager's misspent weekend relate to your business today? Because a simple phrase—or in this case, a simple question—can free you and the people around you. It will help everyone achieve things that you never thought they could achieve. It will cause tidal waves of happiness and accountability. It will change behavior and force people to think and act for themselves. It will get people to imagine possibilities and maybe even weep at missed opportunities. This is fact. These four words are worth the price of this book. If you use this one question, these four simple words, you can change the course of your company's future.

"What do you think?"

That's right: **"What do you think?"** It's the single most powerful question in the history of management training and employee development. It's direct, it's open-ended, it's challenging; and it's a chance for an employee to tell you something you don't know. It's a chance for your employee to tell you what he or she is thinking about the job, how to do the job better, and/or how to make the job more valuable.

"What do you think?" opens doors that you'll never open by yourself, allows you to tap into a completely different brain, and provides a completely different perspective than your own.

Most importantly, it says, "I trust you."

I know a guy whose boss gave him no trust at all. His boss was a dreadful combination of Helicopter Management and Seagull Management. His boss would constantly hover over my friend, telling him how to do his job and giving advice that was 180-degrees different than the advice he gave an hour earlier.

Day in and day out, the boss drove my friend crazy with his micromanaging, to the point where my friend's number one project every day became looking for a new job; it certainly wasn't fulfilling the description for the job he held.

When he told me about what was going on at work, I asked him, "What do you think?" My friend looked at me like I had three eyes. "What do you think?" I asked again.

He told me that he didn't think in his job; he just did whatever his boss wanted him to do.

So I dug a little deeper. I asked him to tell me if he could do his job better if his boss just got out of his office, quit calling him every five minutes with tips, and just got out of his hair. My friend said enthusiastically, "Absolutely!"

I told my friend that he should tell his boss to ask all his direct reports the most important question in business: **"What do you think?"**

Truth Grenade: Training yourself to use "What do you think" is much, much harder than you could ever imagine. Write it down on a piece of paper, and stick it in front of your face to use every day.

A couple weeks later, my friend called me to say he had a new job and that his boss was a new man.

"Why?" I asked.

"When I went in to give my two-week notice, he was stunned. But since I was liberating myself from his shackles, I was able to speak freely. I told him he was a lousy manager, told him that he instilled no trust in his employees, and that he should ask people—just once—what they think."

Asking that simple question showed the boss that his employees really do have some good ideas. They really can think for themselves. They really can make the business more productive with their ideas and initiatives. The atmosphere at the company was changing just about as quickly as the boss used to change the direction he gave to his employees...and my friend was having some regrets about leaving.

"What do you think?" tells your employee that you want his or her input, that you trust his or her thinking and that you want him or her to *do some thinking*.

It also helps solve some of the world's most compelling problems—like all of your employee's problems.

We recently worked with a management team that operates a small business, which requires its salespeople to be out on a pre-determined route every day of the week. The salespeople drive from stop to stop, visiting their customers to fill their orders that will be delivered by a truck the next day.

The supervisory team's *Role* is to guide, mentor, manage, and motivate the sales team to ensure that the mundane replication of this job doesn't cause sluggish sales or negligent behavior. Basically, they need to babysit.

During the course of my work with this client, I spent a day with one of their supervisors, riding on a "typical" Tuesday, to do some in-market coaching and get a better feel for the challenges the supervisors were facing. Upon exiting the building and heading toward our transportation for the day, it started. His phone rang. I could obviously only hear one side of the conversation, but it went something like this:

"Yep; yep; yep. Tell him that's a deal, but he needs to take seventeen next week. If he's willing to do that, we can get it done. Great. Thanks."

"Hmmm," I wondered to myself, "what's happening?"

Once again, before we even sat in our seats for the day, his phone rang again. A similar situation:

"Hey. Okay. Well, I think that sounds good. I'm out in the market today, and we can stop by to talk to him about that. Yup. Okay. We should be there no later than 3:00."

Again, I'm wondering what's happening.

By noon, the phone had rung no less than thirty-five times. Each time, the supervisor gave endless direction and was required to do an endless amount of follow up, causing duplication in work and escalating amounts of unnecessary communication. Come to find out that each of the supervisors receives somewhere in the neighborhood of sixty-five to seventy-five calls in a typical day. These weren't calls from vendors or suppliers—and certainly not from customers with orders—but from the salespeople asking questions about how to do their jobs...the jobs they were hired and paid very well to do.

By 1:00 that day, my stomach was growling louder than a howler monkey's jungle cry; so I asked my guide if we could stop for lunch.

Over lunch I proceeded to inquire about the phone calls he got that day and how he manages those calls. I said, "What if I could help you manage your day to give you four extra hours, help you motivate your employees, and improve your communication so that you don't have to do everything yourself? Does that sound like something you'd be interested in?"

Of course, any fool is going to say "yes"...you'd think.

With some hesitation, the supervisor looked at me and said, "No way you can do that. I've been doing this job for twelve years. I've looked at every possible angle, done everyone's job two times over, and there's no way you can save me even fifteen minutes."

With that I threw out a challenge. I said, "Here's what I want you to do. The next phone call that comes in, I want you to ask your sales rep what he or she thinks is the solution, before you give them the answer."

He looked at me as if I had just dropped the ball at first base. "What? You want me to ask them what they think is the solution? What if they don't get it right? Then what?"

"Well, then," I said, "you help them to see what the right answer is; but you're not allowed to give it to them. And if you can do this the rest of the day, I'll see to it that you get an extra day off when you want it. And the best part about it—if you do it correctly, when you return to work after that day off, your salespeople won't even know you were gone. And your phone won't ring once. Sound like a deal?"

Still with an enormous amount of skepticism, he said to me, "Well, what if they do get it right; why do they need me?"

And there it was.

This supervisor and his peers at this small bread company all felt they couldn't teach anyone what they knew about the job that might improve their performance, because they were afraid of being replaced by someone else. They kept all the decision-making authority so close that no one but they could have any jurisdiction when it came to making decisions. This is the exact reason he was receiving so many phone calls in a day and why he had to waste his time and his employees' time explaining and re-explaining what needed to be done.

So I challenged him again. And this time he bit. "Ask whoever calls you with a question about what he should do regarding an issue or a price discussion with his customer, what *he* thinks is the solution. If he comes up with the right answer, congratulate him. If he comes up with the wrong one, guide him down the path to see if he can solve the problem himself."

And that's what the supervisor did.

We hopped back in the car and jetted off to our next account visit. Within four minutes, the phone rang; it was a sales rep with a problem. I asked the supervisor if he could put the phone on speaker mode, so I could hear both sides of the conversation. It went something like this:

Sales rep: "Hey, I'm over here at the new Loaf and Jug on 8th. They want to know if we can put one of those inflatables on the roof for their grand opening. I told them I had to ask you first.

Me (whispering): "Ask him what he thinks he ought to do."

Supervisor: "Well, what do you think? It's a lot of work to get it up there and manage it. Do you think it's worth it?"

Sales rep: Silence.

Supervisor: "Hello?"

Sales rep: "Well, ahhhh, I don't know. I guess so. I think it would be a great way to show the account we want his business, and we could sure move some bread."

Me (whispering again): "Ask him if he thinks we can get another display if we bring in the inflatable."

Supervisor: "Do you think he would give us another end-cap if we brought in the inflatable?"

Sales rep: "I'll ask."

Supervisor: "I think you have your answer then."

Me (still whispering): "Now tell him he did a good job."

Supervisor: "Great job! Next time this happens, you don't have to ask—you know the answers. You always do."

This chain of events really did happen. What's better is that I was able to show the supervisor that, if he empowered his employees by asking them their opinions, it gave the subordinates a chance to use their brains and, therefore, learn something for the *next time.*

I'm also not suggesting that you walk into one of your employees' offices and, completely out of the blue, yell, "WHAT DO YOU THINK?"

At that point, the employee will probably be thinking, "I think you'd better get a hold of your meds." But if you nurture an environment where people are encouraged to tell you what they think, you can avoid leading a team of people who just sit back and let you, the leader, make decisions for them.

"What do you think?" invites responsibility to become a part of your employees' job descriptions, even if those employees are young people just starting out.

29

OPEN-BOOK MANAGEMENT

JACK Stack is the legendary CEO of Springfield Remanufacturing Company, known as SRC Holdings, and author of the book *The Great Game of Business*. In 1983, Mr. Stack and a dozen other managers put together $100,000 and secured an $8.9 million loan in order to take over this troubled, nine-year-old division of International Harvester. The company, an engine-rebuilding business, had barely weathered the difficult economic times of the late 1970s and early 1980s. Its debt-to-equity ratio was 89:1,[20] and its stock price was ten cents per share.[21] Stack immediately implemented Open-Book Management, a style of management that appeals to each employee's importance and contribution to the company.

"When you appeal to the highest level of thinking, you get a highest level of performance," insists Stack.[22]

20 srcholdings.com/
21 newstreaming.com/about/src-companies/
22 greatgame.com/tour/what-is-it/

Employees who constantly ask themselves, "What would I do differently?" are employees who are stepping over the threshold that separates them from highest-level thinking and highest-level performance. "When employees think, act, and feel like owners...everybody wins," he states.[23]

Open-Book Management isn't necessarily about showing employees all the spreadsheets and calculations that take place in the Accounting Department; rather, it's about making sure that employees understand the critical numbers, the numbers that they need to know in order to make a difference individually and as a part of a team.[24]

Stack and his management team began their stewardship of SRC by realizing that most employees in the business world never see any of their company's performance numbers. Eventually, employees become numb about where their jobs fit in a company and how they can positively affect the company's fortunes. He cited a survey in which sixty-six percent of employees expressed interest in how their company was doing financially, and seventy-five percent of respondents pledged to work harder and smarter if they could understand their company's financial statements.[25] So SRC employees were allowed to see the company's

---

23 greatgame.com/about/

24 greatgame.com/tour/what-is-it/

25 greatgame.com/about/

finances, including collective employee compensation (individual compensation should never be shared); and that helped them understand how even the smallest decisions could positively or negatively affect the bottom line.

Before long, SRC was heading in the right direction, with annual sales of $42 million in 1986.[26] The stock price hit thirteen dollars per share in 1988[27]; and SRC continued to grow, diversify its product base, and hire more people.

One area into which SRC Holdings delved was management training, showing other companies that their employees will support what they help create. Through the "Get in the Game Workshop," Stack and others have helped companies like Cal-Tex Protective Coatings, Virginia Farm Bureau Insurance®, and Federal Companies understand the advantages of Open-Book Management that he trumpeted in his first book.[28] He calls The Great Game of Business "...a process, a pattern, a system, a strategy, a way of thinking..."[29] and insists that a company that wants to realize the benefits of being Open-Book needs to work the process every day. If a company works the process, the results will come.

---

26 fundinguniverse.com/company-histories/SRC-Holdings-Corporation-Company-History.html
27 wikipedia.org/wiki/Springfield_ReManufacturing
28 www.greatgame.com/resources/case-studies/
29 www.greatgameuk.com/tour/learn-it/

It all starts with the right leadership and the ability to share the *Why* with employees before ever sharing the *How*. Then open the books and teach the numbers, apply "High Involvement Planning," and focus on the critical number. Is the critical number a certain cost savings? Is it a certain sales goal? Is it a manufacturing output number? Whatever the critical number is, make sure it's the focus of the employee's work so that the employee acts on the right drivers to achieve that number.

If the employee is onboard with that thinking, has a stake in the outcome, keeps score, and "follows the action," that employee will understand how whatever actions he or she takes affects the company as a whole. That knowledge will allow him or her to work toward a positive result.

Finally, if leadership creates an early "win" for the employee, the effect the employee has will be easy to see.[30]

Open-Book Management may not be for every business, but there's no denying that it provides an opportunity for an employee to do more than a job. An employee has a mission when he works in a company that practices Open-Book Management, and that mission guides his or her behavior on the job. That's the key to success.

---

30 www.jimcollins.com/article_topics/articles/good-to-great.html

---

Truth Grenade: You think that Open-Book Management is a way for everyone in your company to know what others are making. Think again.

So what does success look like at SRC? Today the company has more than 1,000 "engaged" employees, seventeen business units across a variety of industries, $300 million in annual sales, and a stock price of $199 per share.

30

FINDING YOUR REPLACEMENT

WHEN it comes to building an organization of *Owners*, not *Renters*, there is no more powerful tool than asking someone to be you. No, I'm not talking about the well-worn expression, "Hey, buddy, walk a mile in my shoes." I'm talking about making sure that the people who work for you do whatever they do <u>at least</u> as well as you would if you were in their position.

Remember what I highlighted about Chipotle's promotion policy at the end of Part I? Not only does an employee with the company have to show that he or she is ready to take on more responsibility, the employee has to train someone to take the position he or she is vacating. Basically, the promoted employee has to find a new him or her in order to be promoted.

A few years ago, a consultant friend of mine sat down to lunch with a new client. My friend's new client had invited his top three managers to join them and discuss the upcoming projects as a group. When the five of them assembled, my friend took note that there was the CEO, his V.P. of Sales, his V.P. of Operations, and his General Manager. "Makes sense," he said to himself. "Good to be talking to the decision makers."

Shortly after the proper introductions were made, something struck my friend right between the eyes: he was the youngest person at the table...and not by just a few years either. It wasn't a guess; it was obvious. He was the youngest person at the table by at least a generation. No, he didn't blurt out, "So, how old are you coots?" or "Tell me, exactly how was business during the Jefferson Administration?"

But he did have to remind himself that he was being brought in to solve a myriad of problems that these men said they were having with their business, problems that he could see right in front of him.

Truth Grenade: You might be the old coot in this story.

That's why his first question to the group was, "So...who's going to replace each of you?"

There was silence...stunned silence...all around the lunch table. His new clients looked at him like he'd just asked to see pictures of their wives without makeup. The General Manager looked at him like he'd asked to see pictures of his wife without makeup or clothing.

Needless to say, the relationship wasn't off to a good start. And it didn't get any better as it became obvious to my friend that his clients hadn't developed or trained anyone to take over the business. As they saw it, the business was them. They were the business. When one of them decided to retire or was forced to retire, the part of the business for which that particular person was responsible would fall apart. There was no succession plan.

What happened next almost made my friend fall out of his seat. After stammering around for a few minutes trying to answer the question, the V.P. of Sales spoke up with such an air of self-importance that my friend said he thought he was dealing with a bunch of U.S. Senators.

"Replace <u>me</u>?" said the man. "Who will replace me? I'm irreplaceable."

At that exact moment my consultant buddy knew he had his work cut out for him.

TRUTH GRENADE: Chances are you have absolutely no idea who will be replacing you in your present position. But you should...

Succession is not just for geriatric businessmen who think they're irreplaceable. It's for twenty-something administrative assistants. It's for thirty-two-year-old H.R. representatives. It's for middle-aged bread supervisors. Succession is a vital part of any business, if that business is to survive.

It's all about developing people. And since businesses are all about people and relationships between people, a person who's being groomed to accept more and more responsibility is a person who's helping push the business's mission forward. That's a person who is a future *Job Owner.*

Some people in leadership, like my friend's new clients, act like training someone to take over for them is akin to a catcher telling the opposing team's batter what pitch is coming.

Finding your replacement falls under the "Grow Or Die" category. A business that grows is succeeding. A business that doesn't grow is dying. Like the economy, a business does not stand still. So if you're not looking for a replacement for you, someone who can do your job as well as or better than you can, you're not looking to make an improvement in your business.

When you find someone who can replace you, you find someone who is ready to become an *Owner*. You open up a door for that person, one that lets him or her see that there's so much more to master, and that the company wants and expects the person to master it. When the employee walks through that door, he or she is on the way to becoming a *Job Owner*, someone who takes responsibility to learn more, do more, and be more valuable...fully understanding that company leadership expects that.

Better yet, the employee is ready to find a better way to get something done without having to be told how.

Think about it this way:

You know that you bring a certain amount of value to your company. If you identify someone who can be your replacement, you will have found someone who can bring just as much value to your company as you bring and effectively double that value. What could be better than that?

Well, how about having a staff full of people who bring great value to your company finding their own replacements? Wouldn't that effectively double the value of your company again?

Before you start thinking about Mini-Me, the character Vern Troyer played in the *Austin Powers* movies, consider that your business is probably not trying to extort *"one million dollars"* from the world's superpowers. You're not looking for a Mini-Me. You're looking for a person who exhibits the skills you have and possesses the moxie to hone them, use them, and turn them into value for your company, creating more *Owners* simultaneously.

It doesn't have to be a single person who can be your replacement. It could be two people who can both fulfill your responsibilities. If you have an entire staff that could become your replacement, you should feel blessed. You have a group that's ready to bring plenty of new value to your company. All they need is to be allowed to do it.

How do you do it? You bring people in who are more than caretakers for their positions. You challenge an employee who earns $35,000 per year to make his or her job worth

$40,000. You should surround yourself with people who want to move up, intend to move up, and are willing to do what it takes to move up.

If you think you're irreplaceable—and if you think you are the business—you're stuck in a business that's gone just about as far as it can go. You're probably chasing people out of your organization that could be your replacement and could help your company reach a higher level of performance and earnings. Great companies become that way because the people who work there are allowed to do more than their predecessors did; they're allowed to be their predecessors' replacements.

Advertising legend, David Ogilvy, once said, "First, make yourself a reputation for being a creative genius. Second, surround yourself with partners who are better than you are. Third, leave them to go get on with it."[31]

Now, not everyone in the advertising business is a creative genius. But many people who run smart businesses have made those companies better by avoiding the almost natural aversion to placing smarter, more competent people in positions where they can eventually overtake them. The best companies in the world became the best companies

---

31 problogger.net/archives/2011/02/02/10-david-ogilvy-quotes-that-could-revolutionize-your-blogging/

in the world not because the founders and owners were brilliant, but because they were smart enough to hire their replacements and let them "go get on with it."

Too many people look at an underling who could possibly replace them as a threat. That's certainly the kind of attitude my friend encountered with his older-than-dirt clients; they'd chased off numerous employees who'd moved up the ladder and put themselves in a position to replace one of these gentlemen. Some employees had been fired, and others had left of their own volition. Either way, the company was not succeeding; and now these four businessmen were turning to a consultant nearly half their age to tell them why their business was failing after so many prosperous years. My friend had to bite his tongue in order not to blurt out: "There are four reasons why your business is crumbling, and they're all sitting at this table with me."

If you're in leadership, you need to be on the constant lookout for your replacement. Why? Because if you're in leadership, you need to lead the charge when it comes to business development. You need to be constantly on the lookout for new ways that your business can expand. You need to be looking for opportunities.

If your business card carries "S.V.P. of New Business," or "President," or some other important-sounding title, you need to be looking beyond your company's walls in your day-to-day life. Your responsibility to your company and the people who work for you is to let them do the jobs for which they were hired. If you've hired, trained, and staffed correctly, they should have no problem fulfilling the day-to-day operations of your company. That leaves you to spearhead ways for your company to grow, including seeking out a replacement for you.

It's a simple human desire for people to want more. People want to do more, to attain more, to enjoy more, and to get more. A business is in the business of helping clients and customers get "more" of whatever it is a particular business offers. A consumer who wants a more refreshing drink can turn to the Pepsi-Cola that Walter Mack made a household name. Had he not taken the initiative to make Pepsi grow, many other people's lives would be less enjoyable now.

And they'd be parched.

The beauty of finding your replacement is what happens without words—trust. It says, "I trust you. I believe in you. You are good enough to be me, maybe better."

If your organization does not have a formal mentor program, you're missing the boat. That's because creating a formal succession planning process is one of the keys to building an organization full of *Owners*.

Here is what a succession plan should look like in your organization:

Step 1 – Identify your company's future leadership requirements.

- You do that by identifying where your results are today and if you're hitting your goals. If you're not, then what will the coming years look like?
- Evaluate your current organizational structure. Is it helping you or hindering you from succeeding?
- Evaluate the members of your current leadership team. Are they meeting your expectations and helping the business accomplish its objectives?

Step 2 – Define the best leadership style for your company.

- Not all organizations are the same. Some require a heavy-handed style where power is needed at the top. Perhaps your organization succeeds better with a cooperative style, where decisions are made as a group, where the opinions of others are shown ostentatious value. Regardless, determine what stage your company is currently in, and find the best leadership style to meet your needs.

Step 3 – Identify all current and potential leaders.

- Using a tool like *9 Box Grid*, map both the performance and potential of all employees. Promote those who should be promoted, improve those who need improvement, and move out those that should be moved out.

Step 4 – Identify any leadership gaps, and develop "succession-aires" for critical roles.

- Start with your most important management positions, and identify a minimum of two successors. Move on to all key managers in all areas of your company.

Step 5 – Develop career-planning goals for potential leaders.

- Future leaders need development plans. Use an Individual Development Plan where the future leader identifies his or her own job competencies and fills the holes they believe need development.

Step 6 – Develop the roadmap for future leaders.

- A road map lays out the formal training of your future leaders. It will identify the courses or learning programs that your future leader(s) should accomplish in a given period.

Step 7 – Develop retention programs for current and future leaders.

- Once you have identified your future leaders, you want to be certain they are there for a long time. In order of importance, here is a list of top retention tools:
    - Salary increases
    - Bonuses
    - Promotions
    - Autonomy
    - Public praise
    - Private praise
    - Stock options

The job of a consultant is to show his clients how to get more out of their businesses. After much time and many meetings, my friend was able to shift his client's thinking. He was able to convince them to stop using rear-view management—constantly looking at what their employees were doing and interfering with day-to-day operations—

and start looking out at the horizon to find opportunities that could help the company grow in the years ahead, while allowing their employees to do the jobs for which they were hired. In the subsequent years, employees stayed onboard, were developed, and allowed to *own* their jobs.

Best of all, the company started growing again. In fact, for the first time in years, business is...well...**Blooming**.

CONCLUSION

31

NOW WHAT?

HELPING your employees become *Job Owners* is not the easiest thing to do. As an employer, I know that. *Job Ownership* is simply not a concept that many people know or understand.

Frankly, I think it's a concept that worries a lot of business leaders. Leaders are too often afraid of an employee who might eclipse them in knowledge, effectiveness, and value to the company. That sort of leadership only serves to suppress the overall value of the company.

I think that having a staff full of *Job Owners* is the best thing you, as a leader, can do to make your business as effective and profitable as it can be. And in today's business climate, you need every advantage you can get.

To illustrate how you can help the people on your staff to *stop thinking like employees* and start thinking like

Owners, I have used a lot of stories. Oftentimes, the best way to illustrate a concept—especially one as uncommon as *Job Ownership*—is by telling a story. Readers often see something that reminds them of themselves in stories, and I expect you found yourself in a few that are in this book.

Perhaps you were a young route driver twenty-five years ago, constantly stuck in the left-hand turn lane. Maybe you've had to replace one mail kid after another in your office, because the job was seemingly so thankless. Or you may have watched someone perform his or her job— as I did with the kid cooking at the Waffle House—and wondered just how that person did it.

Before I walked into that Waffle House, I had never entertained the thought of *Job Ownership*. But my visit with that cook changed my whole perception of what a job was for most people and what it *can* and *should* be for everyone. It was that realization that has opened up new frontiers to me as an employer, a consultant, and as a trainer of my clients' employees.

Making sure that you have the best employees and the best staff you can possibly have doesn't happen by chance. It doesn't happen due solely to good hiring practices. It happens because you give your people what they need to succeed, you provide them the direction required, you show them the *Why* and the *What* of their jobs, and you help them to become *Job Owners*. It happens because you have convinced the people who work for you to *stop thinking like an employee* and be an *Owner*.

If you want that for your company, look in the mirror. It's all up to you.

BIO

Matt Dahlstrom is a widely-respected speaker, author, and highly sought consultant on employee engagement and owner of the BLOOM Group. He writes the popular blog Inspire Ownership at Work and can be found inspiring leaders to create their own culture of ownership.

Matt lives in Denver with his wife and two sons.

inspire others.
www.MattDahlstrom.com